THE

BOY SCOUTS

An American Adventure

Robert W. Peterson

AMERICAN HERITAGE

New York

Distributed by Houghton Mifflin Company, Boston

Library of Congress Cataloging in Publication Data

Peterson, Robert, 1925–
    The Boy Scouts.

    Includes index.
    1. Boy Scouts of America.   I. Title.
HS3313.P485   1984   369.43′0973   84-16748
ISBN 0-8281-1173-1

Printed in the United States of America

Designed by Blackbirch Graphics

*Scouts belonging to the Order of the Arrow hold a ceremony welcoming new
members around a New Jersey campfire in the 1940's.*

Table of Contents

As this history of the first 75 years of the BSA was going to press, more than 22,000 Boy Scouts from all over our land were preparing to attend the 1985 National Scout Jamboree at Fort A. P. Hill in historic Virginia. Every participant will be immersed in an unforgettable experience, one that will deepen as the years flow by. Can you imagine that some of these Scouts who will celebrate the movement's 75th anniversary will also be around for the Boy Scouts of America's 150th birthday in 2060?

I feel certain that there will be Boy Scouts around as long as our country continues to be great. Right now, the membership of the Boy Scouts of America is growing, although the numbers dipped drastically in the seventies. But we're back on the upward trail. For example, in 1984 we adopted Varsity Scouting—a program designed specifically for boys from 14 through 17—after it had been field tested for 7 years. By the time this program was officially introduced at the Biennial National Meeting in Salt Lake City, more than 20,000 boys were Varsity Scouts.

Our Tiger Cub program for 7-year-old boys has taken off like a rocket. The Tiger Cubs will supplement the regular Cub Scout activities, offering another source of membership in much the same way that the Webelos program helps in the growth of Boy Scouting. Boy Scout and Cub Scout membership suffered the most loss in the seventies.

A really bright picture is the continuing expansion of the Explorer program for high school–age boys and girls. In 1983 the membership exploded by 25 percent. In large measure this increase was due to the popularity of Career Awareness Exploring. This program is a valued support to schools across our country as thousands invite the BSA in to bring definitive career information to high school students.

The total BSA membership—this also includes adults—is just below the 5 million mark as we observe our diamond jubilee. With the continuing support of Americans, it should go higher.

Edward C. Joullian III
President, BSA

In the section containing memorable dates in U.S. history in the 1984 *World Almanac and Book of Facts*, there's only one listing for the year 1910. The seven-word entry reads, "Boy Scouts of America founded Feb. 8." Surely something else of significance occurred in 1910, but the truth is that whatever happened could not have affected life in these United States more than Scouting has.

The period before World War I was a transitional time wavering between the old and the new. In 1909, for example—the year before William Boyce and his friends incorporated the BSA—Admiral Robert Peary went by dogsled to the North Pole. In 1911—the year after Scouting began—pioneer aviator C. P. Rodgers startled the nation by flying from New York to Pasadena in 82 hours and 4 minutes. His flight was a remarkable feat, even though he left New York on September 17 and arrived in Pasadena on November 5.

The world was really different in 1910. The words "Boy Scout" were not common then. Recognition came later. Scouting was famous enough in 1915 to induce the most famous American band leader ever, John Philip Sousa, to write a march dedicated to the Boy Scouts of America. The public came to recognize that Scouts always were ready to help others and always were prepared for whatever happened.

The year 1928 demonstrated that our motto, "Be Prepared," was not idle words. Three Eagle Scouts accompanied explorers Martin and Asa Johnson on their rugged safari to Tanganyika. A fourth Eagle sailed with Commodore Richard Byrd to Antarctica, an experience that today would be comparable to recruiting a Scout to spend time on a space satellite.

No one has asked a Scout to fly into space, but former Scouts made our first thrusts away from the earth—and some of them walked on the moon. Two Boy Scouts became President of the United States. The Boy Scouts of America has been woven into the fabric of America. We are part of the tapestry of history, because millions of Americans have made us so.

J. L. Tarr
Chief Scout Executive, BSA

All Together Now

As the Boy Scouts of America approached its 75th anniversary—which this delightful book commemorates—a monumental analysis of all aspects of the BSA reminded us that the movement's future is bound forever and inextricably to its ability to instill values in the hearts and minds of our young people. This study, which we called Shaping Tomorrow, also suggested that the Boy Scouts of America must prepare these youngsters to make ethical choices over their lifetimes while achieving their full potential.

In effect, the hundreds of volunteer and professional leaders involved in the Shaping Tomorrow project declared, it is our duty to prepare our youth members for the responsibilities of citizenship in their great republic. That is the challenge the BSA faces—and accepts—as it moves toward the 21st century.

The values that we shall continue to share with our young people revolve around a belief in our Scout Law, which proclaims a Scout is trustworthy, loyal, helpful, friendly, courteous, kind, obedient, cheerful, thrifty, brave, clean, and reverent, and around the Scout Oath, which pledges a Scout "... to do my duty to God and my country and to obey the Scout Law..." while helping other people as he keeps himself "... physically strong, mentally awake and morally straight."

As a result of the Shaping Tomorrow studies, we clearly understand that the future of the BSA is best expressed by the following mission statement: *It is the mission of the Boy Scouts of America to serve others by helping to instill values in young people and, in other ways, prepare them to make ethical choices over their lifetime in achieving their full potential.*

Sanford N. McDonnell
President-elect, BSA

Avid outdoorsmen throughout their history, Boy
Scouts learn logging at a New York camp in
1912 (inset) and at Philmont Scout Ranch today.

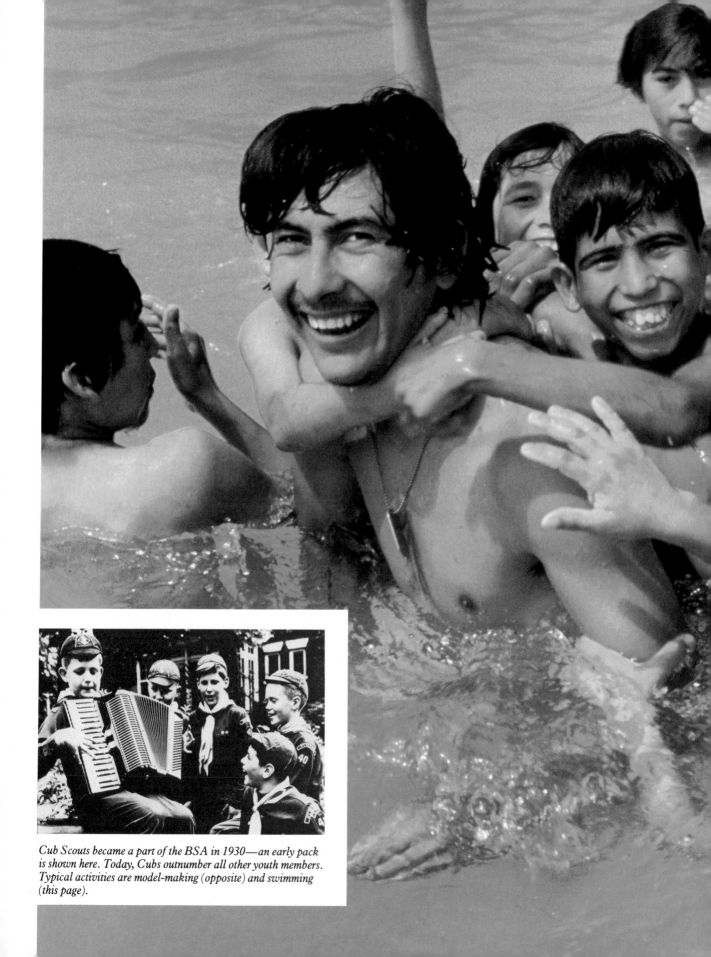

Cub Scouts became a part of the BSA in 1930—an early pack is shown here. Today, Cubs outnumber all other youth members. Typical activities are model-making (opposite) and swimming (this page).

Older teenagers take part in the BSA's Explorer program and develop valuable skills in such pursuits as aviation (above), mountaineering (left), and fire fighting (right).

1
The Fathers of Scouting

It is the exception when we see a boy respectful of his superiors and obedient to his parents. It is the rare exception, now, when we see a boy that is handy with tools and capable of taking care of himself under all circumstances. It is the very, very rare exception when we see a boy whose life is absolutely governed by the safe old moral standards. . . . To combat the system that has turned such a large proportion of our robust, manly, self-reliant boyhood into a lot of flat-chested cigarette-smokers, with shaky nerves and a doubtful vitality, I began the Woodcraft movement in America. —Ernest Thompson Seton, 1910

AT THE DAWN of the 20th century, an American boy's life was either full of drudgery or idyllic, depending on his family's circumstances. During the decade before the founding of the Boy Scouts of America in 1910, the families of a handful of industrialists lived sumptuously while four-fifths of the population skirted the edges of poverty or were enmeshed in it. Simultaneously, the emerging and vital middle class was pretty comfortable.

For the sons of factory supervisors, white-collar workers, and professional men, life had a Tom Sawyer quality. After school, a middle-class boy might have some home chores to do but he had time for play, too —baseball, perhaps, or fishing and skating as the seasons allowed.

Children looked mostly to each other for entertainment. The first municipal playgrounds were beginning to appear in some cities. There were weekly band concerts, church socials, and men's baseball games to watch; Little

These Pennsylvania Scouts built this bridge in 1912, enabling them to walk from camp to a nearby trolley line.

Robert Stephenson Smyth Baden-Powell, founder of Scouting, painted by Benjamin Eggleston.

Patriotically attired, these children await a parade in 1910.

League baseball and other organized sports for boys were far in the future. Vaudeville was thriving, and the first movies, called nickelodeons, were being shown in amusement parlors for any boy lucky enough to have a nickel. Radio and television were merely gleams in the eyes of scientists.

If a boy's family was churchgoing and Protestant, he might join Christian Endeavor, the Epworth League, the Baptist Young People's Union of the Southern Baptist convention, or perhaps one of the more colorful groups with names like the Circle of Ten, Knights of King Arthur, the Princely Knights of Character Castle, Brotherhood of St. Andrew, Knights of the Holy Grail, or the Young Crusaders of the Church Temperance League. Among organizations with secular as well as religious aims, the largest was the Young Men's Christian Association, which had branches in most cities

and many towns. For boys who admired soldiers, there was the Boys' Brigade, a paramilitary organization with liberal doses of religious training.

Boys with an outdoor bent could fish in clean streams and hike in woods and meadows that lay even on the fringes of the great cities. In some ways, the boys' world of those days seemed not greatly different from the lot of youth today to whom the outdoors may be available. Julian H. Salomon, a long-time Scout and Scouter whose preteen years were spent in New London, Conn., and Brooklyn, N.Y., recently recorded: "I wouldn't say there was anything unusual about our life then from what it would be in a suburb now. I can remember hiking down a creek in Brooklyn and going by old Dutch farms. The southern end of Brooklyn in Canarsie and Flatbush was all undeveloped—still Dutch farms."

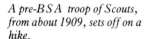

A pre-BSA troop of Scouts, from about 1909, sets off on a hike.

But something was missing, something was changing. As the nation grew increasingly urbanized, many youngsters could no longer roam freely, ride a horse, swim, or learn how to handle tools and manage domestic animals. Observers who remembered America's rural past worried that boys circa 1900 were no longer physically strong, self-reliant, and resourceful as their pioneer ancestors had been. So two special men, Ernest Thompson Seton and Daniel Carter Beard, resolved to address the disturbing and unequal situation of American boys.

These two men played critically important roles in the foundation of Scouting within the existing structures of early 20th-century life in America. They were perhaps minor figures among the great men and women called Progressives who pressed for social reform in this transitional era. Nonetheless the Boy Scouts of America and the organization's predecessor in England were notable by-products of the reformist urge.

Seton and Beard—along with renowned Progressives like Theodore Roosevelt (who later became a staunch advocate of Scouting and honorary Chief Scout Citizen), Robert M. La Follette, and journalist Lincoln Steffens —were looking at a changing youth population, an entire nation struggling to adapt to its new status as the world's leading industrial power. A wave of immigration, mostly from southern and eastern Europe, was bringing hordes of workers to live in poverty in big cities. Many metropolises were rife with corruption. At least l.7 million children between the ages of 10 and 15 were employed full time in field, factory, and mine. More than half of them were in agriculture, some laboring 12 hours a day. Their work was at least in a healthful atmosphere, but the same couldn't be said for the 20,000 children in southern cotton mills or the 25,000 boys in mines and quarries. Ernest Thompson Seton was already famous as a naturalist, wildlife artist, author, and lecturer when he determined to devote his energies to the looming problem of American youth. His initial contribution to the cause was the establishment of the Woodcraft Indians, which he founded in 1902.

Born in England in 1860, Seton had spent his boyhood on a farm in the wilderness of Ontario, Canada, and his late teen years in Toronto. Having shown artistic talent, he was sent to London at 19 to study art at the Royal Academy. At 2l he was back in Canada, tramping the wilds of Manitoba. He soon began making a name as a naturalist and painter of wildlife, and when he was 26 years old Seton published *Mammals of Manitoba*, the first of 46 books.

In 1898 his reputation was enhanced by publication of his classic *Wild Animals I Have Known*, and he had established himself on a small estate in Cos Cob, Conn. When he moved into the striking house he had designed, neighborhood boys decided to test this 6-foot, bespectacled newcomer by defacing his fence and perpetrating other mischief. Instead of calling the law, Seton invited the boys to camp on his property.

With the artist as camp chief, the boys had a grand time hiking, learning camping skills, studying trees and wildlife, and hearing Seton tell gripping tales of the American Indian. He could weave a spell around adults, too. Lincoln Steffens described Seton thus: "Tall, handsome, poet-like, he was animal-like, too. I suppose 'child-like' is the word most people would to use to describe the animal sense he had for springs, trees, plants and shady nooks."

Out of Seton's first camp for boys grew the Woodcraft Indians. In 1902 he wrote a series of articles about outdoor life for the *Ladies' Home Journal*, and that July he formed the first tribe of Woodcraft Indians at the Fresh Air and Convalescent Home for slum children in Summit, N.J.

The Woodcraft Indians offered badges for learning various useful skills, mostly in the outdoors. There was no uniform but homemade Indian headdresses or sashes served to display honors. Although there were nominal headquarters in Greenwich, Conn., it appears that Seton handled the correspondence himself. William W. Edel, who was growing up in Baltimore, Md., remembered: "I completed the first four tests and he mailed me four pieces of wampum—sections of shell about an inch square with tiny holes at the corners so they could be sewed onto your jacket. I learned fire-making first, and I got a piece of wampum for that. Then I think I learned how to treat common health complaints—diarrhea, constipation, and so forth—and I wrote a story of how I would treat them, and I got a second piece of wampum," he recalled. "I remember that I was very proud of the fact that these four pieces of wampum entitled me to wear four eagle feathers —turkey feathers, of course—in my Indian headdress."

Ernest Thompson Seton (below), artist and wildlife expert, founded the Woodcraft Indians in 1902 to teach boys about the outdoors. In 1910, he became the first Chief Scout of the BSA and rushed out the organization's first handbook (above).

Julian Salomon was also corresponding with Seton from his New London home, and eventually he was invited to camp at Cos Cob. After he came home, he formed a Woodcraft Indians tribe. "It was just four or five kids in the backyard," he explained. "We went on hikes but we didn't camp overnight. The whole thing really revolved around the camp at Seton's place."

The Woodcraft Indians were not enough to satisfy Salomon's love of the outdoors, so at about the age of 10 he joined the Sons of Daniel Boone, too. This group was the work of Daniel Carter Beard, an illustrator, editor, and author of books for boys. Beard was born in Cincinnati, Ohio, in 1850, son of James H. Beard, a well-known painter. He had enjoyed an active boyhood, full of boisterous games and mischief, in Cincinnati and later in Covington, Ky.

As a young man, Dan Beard became a surveyor with a hobby of painting and drawing from nature. In 1878 he sold a drawing of a fish to *St. Nicholas* magazine, beginning a long career as an illustrator and writer. In his autobiography, Beard wrote that he first became interested in helping boys when he saw New York City newsboys sleeping on stones under a statue of Benjamin Franklin. He turned to writing and illustrating stories for youth for *St. Nicholas*, *Harper's Round Table*, *Youth's Companion*, and other magazines. His best-known illustrations, though, were for the first edition of Mark Twain's *A Connecticut Yankee in King Arthur's Court*.

In June 1905 he founded the Society of the Sons of Daniel Boone through the pages of *Recreation* magazine. Like Ernest Thompson Seton, he was a prolific correspondent, and he promoted the new organization as much by letters to boys as by his magazine writings.

Julian Salomon's Brooklyn group of the Sons of Daniel Boone often hiked but never camped. At the time, Dan Beard was living in Flushing,

N.Y., then a pastoral village on the edge of New York City (now part of the borough of Queens), and after corresponding with Beard, Salomon was invited to visit him.

"He was just great!" Salomon remembered. "He was almost as good as Seton was in dealing with kids. I'd come hiking over to Flushing with some pal, and Lord! he'd welcome us as if we were his long-lost sons. He'd take us into his studio, feed us some pemmican and bring out an old Indian something-or-other and talk about it. He was just a friendly, genial gentleman."

It is not known how many boys were enrolled in the Woodcraft Indians or Sons of Daniel Boone, but probably neither had more than 2,000. Both groups were the products of artists—men of vision and imagination with little interest in administration or record-keeping.

While American boys with a taste for outdoor life were following Seton and Beard, another youth organization was taking shape in the mind of an English war hero named Robert S. S. Baden-Powell. His design would form the foundation of the Boy Scouts of America.

Like his American counterparts, Baden-Powell was a man of many parts —soldier, artist, author, and skilled amateur actor. He was born in London in 1857 to the daughter of a vice-admiral and an Oxford University professor of geometry who died when Robert was 3 years old. As the scion of an upper-middle-class family, Baden-Powell was educated at Charterhouse, a 5-century-old private school. Graduated at 19, he failed the examination for Oxford but earned an Army commission and was assigned to the 13th Hussars, a cavalry regiment then stationed in India, the crown jewel of the British Empire.

For the next 34 years Baden-Powell was a soldier. He fought in Britain's Afghan Wars in 1880–8l and in later campaigns against the Zulus, Ashantis,

Ernest Thompson Seton (far right) and Daniel Carter Beard (second from left) hand out awards to Boy Scouts in Brooklyn, N. Y., in 1912.

and Matabeles in Africa. He developed considerable skill in military surveillance and spying and wrote training manuals on those subjects. Much of his overseas service was in India where he became a skilled horseman, polo player, and devotee of the sport of pigsticking, and won renown as an artist and actor in regimental theatricals.

As the 19th century waned, Baden-Powell was a colonel, on track toward completion of a successful military career that probably would not take him to the top echelons of the British Army but would lead to an honorable retirement in England. Fate had other designs.

In 1899 he was posted to South Africa because war was threatening with the Dutch settlers—called Boers—in the Transvaal Republic. He was ordered to raise two mounted infantry regiments to guard the border between the Transvaal and the British colonies of Rhodesia (now Zimbabwe) and Bechuanaland (now Botswana). When the Boer War began, Baden-Powell was established in headquarters at Mafeking, a sleepy town in Bechuanaland with about 700 soldiers, policemen, and volunteers.

The Boers laid siege to Mafeking with a force of 7,000 men. By guile and ruse, Baden-Powell deceived the Boers into thinking that a major British force was encamped there. Among his innovations during the siege was a uniformed cadet corps of boys who served as messengers, lookouts, and orderlies. For 217 days, Baden-Powell held out while Great Britain held its collective breath. When a British relief force arrived to lift the siege, England went wild in celebration and Baden-Powell became an instant hero.

Mafeking was only a minor chapter in the Boer War, but it changed the life of Robert S. S. Baden-Powell. He was promoted to major general, the youngest of the rank in the Army, and was put in charge of imperial forces in the northwestern Transvaal. Later he was assigned to establish a South African Constabulary to police the defeated Boer territories.

In 1903 he returned to England and was astonished to find that an Army manual he had written was being used by boys for outdoor fun. The book was called *Aids to Scouting*. He had corrected the proofs just before the siege at Mafeking began. Later, excerpts had been published in a magazine called *Boys of the Empire* under the title "The Boy Scouts."

Aids to Scouting had nothing to do with boys; it was a compendium of ideas for training British soldiers to their real tasks in the outposts of empire. Baden-Powell had found that while the average soldier was competent in drill, he knew nothing of living in the open or the skills of military scouting, and he was lost when resourcefulness or initiative was needed. The book suggested ways to train such men in patrols of eight under the close supervision of an officer.

Schoolteachers urged the returning hero of Mafeking to rewrite the book for use by boys, an idea that appealed to him. For most of the preceding 3 decades, though, he had been out of England and knew little of her youth. He also recognized that he had no background in boys' education and training. So with characteristic thoroughness, he set about reading everything he could find that dealt with the training of boys and young men. Among his readings were the codes of King Arthur, the Zulus of Africa, American Indians, Pacific Islanders, the Boys' Brigade in England, the Bushido of the Japanese, Ernest Thompson Seton's *Camp Games*, and Dan Beard's *Boy Pioneers*. But mainly, he said later, his ideas

At the first official Boy Scout Camp, at Silver Bay on Lake George in upstate New York, Dan Beard shows how to throw a tomahawk. The year is 1912.

THE SONS OF DANIEL BOONE

As stated by founder Dan Beard, the purposes of the Society of the Sons of Daniel Boone were: "The elevation of sport, the support of all that tends to healthy, wholesome manliness; the study of woodcraft, outdoor recreation, and fun, and serious work for the making and support of laws prohibiting the sale of game, and the preservation of our native wild plants, birds, and beasts." In addition, Beard hoped to "awaken in the boy of today, admiration for the old-fashioned virtues of American Knights in Buckskin and a desire to emulate them."

In the Sons of Daniel Boone (later called Boy Pioneers) eight boys made up a stockade; four stockades made a fort. Officers bore titles redolent of the frontier. The president was Daniel Boone, and others were called Simon Kenton, Kit Carson, Audubon, Johnny Appleseed, and David Crockett. In his book *The Boy Pioneers*, Beard suggested homemade uniforms in frontiersman style, emblems for officers, and a red, buff, and green flag with a tree, powder horn, bird, and the initials "SDB." The program featured camping skills and outdoor crafts.

centered on his own experience in training soldiers and the South African Constabulary.

Seton had sent Baden-Powell a copy of *The Birch Bark Roll*, his manual for the Woodcraft Indians, which the old soldier evidently found interesting because later Seton said Baden-Powell had acknowledged the gift by writing, "It may interest you to know that I had been drawing up a scheme with a handbook for it, for the education of boys as Scouts, which curiously runs much on the line of yours."

In October 1906, while Seton was on a lecture tour of England, he visited Baden-Powell in London. Seton later wrote that *The Birch Bark Roll* had greatly influenced Baden-Powell. In fact, he concluded that the Englishman appropriated the Woodcraft program nearly in full. "He adopted the Woodcraft scheme of honor badges, with trifling modifications," Seton wrote. "He adopted the totems, etc., under another name."

After meeting Seton, Baden-Powell continued his researches and later that year his thinking had crystallized into a plan. He put it into a paper called "Boy Scouts—A Suggestion," and sent copies to men who might be interested. The plan, he said, aimed "to help in making the rising generation, of whatever class or creed, into good citizens at home or for the colonies." Boy Scouting would "offer instruction in the many valuable qualities which go to make a good Citizen equally with a good Scout." Boy Scout groups would have patrols of six Scouts under a patrol leader, with four to ten patrols making up a troop under a Scout Master.

The replies to his paper were uniformly favorable, and the next step was a field test. In 1907 Baden-Powell recruited 12 boys from the upper class and 9 workingmen's sons from Poole and Bournemouth on England's southern coast and took them camping on Brownsea Island in Poole Harbor. For 2 weeks, from July 29 to August 9, they were given instruction in camp skills, observation and tracking, woodcraft and nature lore, life-saving and first aid, and the virtues of honor, chivalry, and good citizenship. The boys were divided into four patrols which competed in games testing their new knowledge. They lived in Army tents and were fed by Army cooks.

It was a great adventure, one of the campers recalled. "You have to think back to what it was like in those days," said Arthur Primmer, a Poole working-class boy who was 15 when the Brownsea camp was held. "I don't think I'd ever seen a motorcar when we went to Brownsea—no television, no wireless, and everything was primitive compared to what it

Dan Beard's favorite photo shows him seated with Baden-Powell. When it was taken, in 1937, Beard was 86 and Baden-Powell was 80. Both wear the Silver Buffalo, BSA's highest award, around their necks.

A boy dives into a blanket during Scouting's first outing, on England's Brownsea Island in 1907. Baden-Powell invited 21 boys for fun and camping instruction.

is today. Nobody went camping—not boys. The only camping that was done then was by the Army."

The camp was also successful from Baden-Powell's viewpoint, and so he set about putting his ideas into written form. The result was the first Boy Scout manual, called *Scouting for Boys*, published in March 1908. It was a 182-page pocket-size book with drawings by Baden-Powell. Chapters were titled "Scoutcraft," "Campaigning," "Camp Life," "Tracking," "Woodcraft," "Endurance for Scouts," "Chivalry," "Saving Life," and "Our Duties as Citizens," with subchapters called Campfire Yarns. The yarns included directions for living in the outdoors and tales with morals drawn from Baden-Powell's experience and reading. The book also told how to become a Boy Scout and explained the Scout Promise, Law, the motto "Be Prepared," and the Scout sign, salute, and handshake. The suggested uniform, based on Baden-Powell's outfit for the South African Constabulary, included a broad-brimmed hat, loose shirt with neckerchief, shorts, and knee-length stockings with garters.

Copies of *Aids to Scouting* were snapped up by the thousands, and within weeks Scout troops dotted the British isles. *Scouting for Boys* quickly made the transatlantic crossing, too, for by late spring Scouting had made its appearance in the United States and Canada. Boys in North America were no less thrilled by the promise of outdoor adventure, and leaders of boys' work, particularly in YMCA's, were quick to grasp Scouting's potential for training youth.

Claims by several communities to have had the first troop in the United States are shrouded in undocumented legend, but it is known that by early 1910 dozens of troops were flourishing. In the spring of 1908, a lady named Myra Greeno Bass used *Scouting for Boys* to start the Eagle troop in Burnside, a Kentucky mountain town. Her Scouts hiked and may have camped out in the forests around Burnside. In bad weather they gathered in Mrs. Bass's parlor and read *Treasure Island*.

Troops were also formed that year at Fort Leavenworth, Kans., and in Paterson and Montclair, N.J. In Paterson, the moving spirit was Hunter B. Grant, the YMCA's boys' work secretary. In a newspaper interview in 1924, Grant said he decided to try Scouting for YMCA boys after reading *Scouting for Boys*. "We specialized mostly in hiking, camping, and overnight trips, and had a bully good time," he remembered.

Later in 1908 and 1909, troops were organized in Sedalia, Mo., Staten Island, N.Y., Salina, Kans., Pawhuska, Okla., Frankfort, Ky., Buffalo, N.Y., Chicago, and some towns in Michigan. Scouting skills were being taught in YMCA's in New York and Chicago, but it is not known whether troops were started. By the spring of 1910, troops were also operating in Springfield, Mass., Utica, N.Y., Columbus, Ohio, Indianapolis, Boston, and St. Louis.

Some of the early troops grew out of Sunday School classes. Troop 2 of Bloomfield, N.J., began as a religious class in Westminster Church, which brought Scouting into its activities in the spring of 1909. (Troop 2 has been continuously active ever since and is now chartered to the Presbyterian Church on the Green.)

Surviving members of those pioneer troops have fond memories. John L. Johnson, one of 19 boys who made up the first troop in Pawhuska, Okla., in May 1909 remembered that the Scoutmaster was an Englishman, an Episcopal priest named John Mitchell. He had been sent to organize a

The Brownsea campers came from all social strata. At camp's end, their parents visited and observed the skills they'd learned, such as first aid, shown here.

William D. Boyce in 1894.

mission in Pawhuska, a village of 1,300 and home of an Osage Indian agency. The troop did a lot of drilling and some boxing, Johnson recalled. "Mostly we did the same things Boy Scouts do now, hiking and camping and things like that," he said. The Pawhuska troop was uniformed, and the story was that the Reverend Mr. Mitchell had sent to England for the outfits. But photographs show many Scouts in U.S. Army–style jackets and knee breeches, which were not Baden-Powell's recommended wear.

In Chicago, the first known troop was formed on the South Side in August 1909 by another Englishman named O. W. Kneeves. "My brother and I went to the first meeting and I was thrilled by it," Albert W. Patzlaff recalled. The troop had a drill team that did precision marching (but without guns) for lodges and other groups. On Saturdays, the troop learned Scouting skills in and around the fieldhouse at the city's Hamilton Park or went hiking or camping on Chicago's fringes. "We made our own pup tents," Patzlaff said, "and our uniforms were hand-me-down Army uniforms we got from surplus stores."

That Chicago troop had no name or number, and apparently Scoutmaster Kneeves did not immediately enlist in the Boy Scouts of America when it was born in 1910. Patzlaff remembered that his troop marched in the Fourth of July parade that year and met two or three troops from the Woodlawn area. "They said they were Troop No. 1, Troop No. 2," he said. "Well, that didn't go well with our Scoutmaster because he said, 'We were here before you fellows and so we ought to be Troop No. 1.' For maybe a year he didn't line up with the BSA, but when we finally did we were Troop 6 or 8 or 10. I don't remember. The boys didn't care, but the Scoutmaster felt badly about it."

In the fall of 1909, a young Scottish stonecutter named William Milne, who lived in Barre, Vt., brought home a copy of *Scouting for Boys* after a visit to Great Britain. He showed it to his Boys' Brigade group in the Baptist Church and asked whether the boys would like to try Scouting. "We were entranced by his descriptions, and we said yes," remembered Dr. Wallace Watt. Billy Milne's troop hiked and camped, learned first aid and signaling, and played games like Capture the Flag in the Vermont hills. "Scouting was active and outdoors, and we felt we were doing things that were much more useful than what we did in the Boys' Brigade," Dr. Watt said.

In Springfield, Mass., and Utica, N.Y., troops were started by YMCA boys' work secretaries in March 1910. Springfield Secretary Edwin D. Horsfield reported that other troops were forming in three churches and a grammar school. "We have adopted a uniform very much like the English, consisting of a khaki hat, shirt and trousers," he said. "My experience with the boy scout movement in Scotland convinces me that the American boy will take to this even more enthusiastically than those across the water. The American boy lacks discipline, and the Boy Scout movement will certainly furnish this."

In Utica, YMCA Secretary S. S. Aplin reported that his troop went hiking every Saturday and holiday. "The boys are taught to be cheerful and contented under all circumstances, and heavy penalties are given for swearers or grumblers," he said.

THE WOODCRAFT INDIANS

In his handbook for the Woodcraft Indians, Ernest Thompson Seton said the purposes were "the promotion of interests in out-of-door life and woodcraft, the preservaton of wild life and landscape and the promotion of good fellowship among its members. The plan aims to give the young people something to do, something to think about and something to enjoy in the woods, with a view always to character building, for manhood, not scholarship, is the first aim of education." Seton added, "My foundation thought was to discover, preserve, develop, and diffuse" American Indian culture as he perceived it.

The Woodcraft Indians organization called for an adult, the Medicine Man or Guide, to supervise. The members were Braves and were grouped in bands of three to ten boys; each band bore the name of a wild creature and wore its totem. Two or more bands made up a tribe led by a chief. A boy could join at 12 and earn honors or coups by passing various tests.

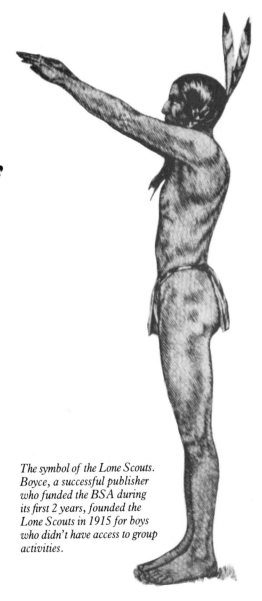

The symbol of the Lone Scouts. Boyce, a successful publisher who funded the BSA during its first 2 years, founded the Lone Scouts in 1915 for boys who didn't have access to group activities.

The early troops took their cues from Baden-Powell's *Scouting for Boys* because there was no semblance of a national movement in the United States. The YMCA men who started most of the early troops saw Boy Scouting merely as a promising adjunct to their programs for boys.

That would soon change. The catalyst was an unlikely figure, a self-made millionaire publisher from Chicago named William Dickson Boyce. He employed from 20,000 to 30,000 boys to sell his publications across the Midwest and parts of the East, but he had never shown concern for their education or training.

Boyce was born to a farm family in Allegheny County, Pa., in 1858. Farming held no attractions for this ambitious lad, and after ending his formal education with 3 years at Wooster (Ohio) Academy, he went to Chicago in 1881 to seek his fortune. He had a gift for making money, and by 1892 he owned the *Chicago Saturday Blade* and *Chicago Ledger*, both circulated widely by his network of enterprising young salesmen. Often featured in his papers were accounts of expeditions he sent all over the world; sometimes he went along and wrote accounts of his exploits as a big game hunter.

He entered the story of Scouting almost by chance in 1909. Boyce's accounts of how it happened vary in details, but all center on a London boy who was to become famous as the Unknown Scout.

Boyce was in London on business in August 1909 en route to British East Africa for a photography and shooting expedition. One afternoon the city was enshrouded in a pea-soup fog. Boyce lost his bearings in the murk and was approached by a boy of about 12 carrying a lantern who offered to guide him to the address he was seeking. When Boyce proffered a shilling tip, the boy replied, "No, sir, I am a Scout. Scouts do not accept tips for courtesies or Good Turns." The American publisher was intrigued, and after he had completed his business, the lad led him to the new British Scout office nearby. There Boyce talked with an official, but probably not Baden-Powell. (William Hillcourt, author of the definitive biography of Baden-Powell, said that almost certainly the two never met.)

During the next 4 months in Africa, Boyce studied the British Scouting materials and accounts of Scouting activities that appeared in English newspapers. He later wrote, "I thought what a wonderful thing it would be for our American boys." On his way back to America in late 1909 or early 1910, he visited Scout headquarters in London again.

The Unknown Scout story is given credence in the first annual report of the Boy Scouts of America, which reported that Scouting "in the present form was brought from England by Mr. W. D. Boyce of Chicago, he being led to do this because of an actual service done by a London Scout." The Unknown Scout was never identified but he was formally enshrined in Scouting's pantheon in 1926 with the award of the second Silver Buffalo, the BSA's highest adult honor for service to boyhood; the first went to Baden-Powell, the third to Boyce.

Boyce came home determined to start Boy Scouting in America. He apparently knew nothing of the troops already operating or of the YMCA's promotion of Scouting.

On February 8, 1910, Boyce filed incorporation papers for the Boy Scouts of America in the District of Columbia. The purpose, he said, "shall be to promote, through organization, and cooperation with other agencies, the ability of boys to do things for themselves and others, to train them in Scoutcraft, and to teach them patriotism, courage, self-reliance, and kindred virtues, using the methods which are in common use by Boy Scouts."

In Weehawken, N. J., in 1908, a pre-BSA Scout gives the salute.

Guidebooks of the
Founding Fathers

SCOUTING
FOR BOYS

BY
BADEN-POWELL

Scouting's first manual was both written and illustrated by Baden- Powell in 1908.

TOMMY THE TENDERFOOT No. 5　　　　**TOMMY SLEEPS OUT**

Plenty of blankets *below*—he'd been told.
But Tommy knew better—and so he got cold.

A Book for Boys

After a training book he had written for soldiers became widely popular among boys, British war hero Robert S. S. Baden-Powell undertook to create a similar book intended for youths. The result, *Scouting for Boys*, appeared in 1908 and quickly became a best-seller in both Britain and the United States, inspiring the formation of dozens of early Scout troops. In 1910, Baden-Powell added an element of humor to the guidebook with the introduction of Tommy the Tenderfoot. Each of Tommy's misadventures—including the error of smoking cigarettes—was underlined with a bright yet cautionary couplet, some of which are shown on this page.

TOMMY THE TENDERFOOT No. 2　　　**TOMMY FELLS A TREE**

Poor Tommy's forgotten to sharpen his axe,
So the tree only suffers a series of whacks.

TOMMY THE TENDERFOOT No. 6　　　　　　**TOMMY BUILDS A FIRE**

On lighting of fires he sets everyone right,
But his own little bonfire refused to ignite.

Three ages of man, Zulu style (above) and British Scout style (right).

Boy Scout

Old Scout

Wolf Cub

A Scout's way (left) and an Indian's way of transporting gear (above).

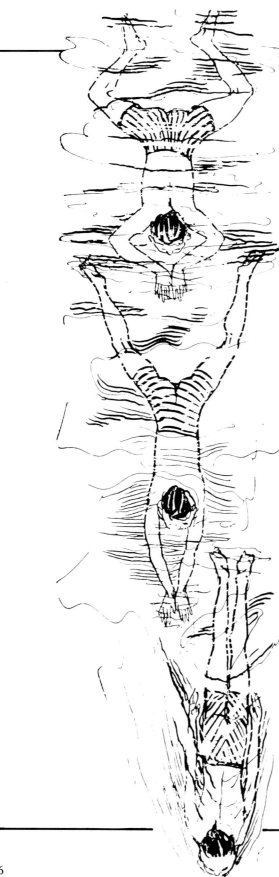

From Dan Beard's Handbook

Daniel Carter Beard was an author and illustrator of books for boys long before he became a pioneering Boy Scout leader. His first volume, *What to Do and How to Do It: The American Boys' Handy Book*, published in 1882, reveals a keen naturalist's and artist's perception of subjects many boys wanted to know about: swimming, camping, spear-throwing, boat and tree-house building, snowball-fort construction, and fishing. Born in 1850, Beard was the son and nephew of prominent American artists and trained at the Art Students' League in New York. His career as a professional illustrator was launched in 1878, when he sold a drawing of a fish to *St. Nicholas* magazine; over the next 50 years, he produced some 20 books for boys, most of them for the Boy Scouts.

The neck hold saves a life.

The broad stroke—"Poses Purposely Exaggerated."

The water swing according to Beard: Construct a set of hoisting shears to prop up a "sweep" at a high angle; nail the bottom of the sweep to a tree, and take off.

Beard's Tree Houses

Beard's books encouraged boys to become not just outdoorsmen but outdoor construction engineers, building a seemingly endless variety of bridges, dams, camps, cabins, docks, boats, rafts, and, in this case, tree houses. His faith in a boy's abilities seems almost limitless—one section of text describing the building of a frame, walls, and a roof for a tree house begins, "The rest of the work is simple." Uncle Dan, as he was called by Scouts and other friends, is best known today as a founder of the Boy Scouts and a naturalist—Mt. Beard, adjoining Mt. McKinley, in Alaska, was named for him. But as an artist, he did the pictures for the first edition of Mark Twain's *A Connecticut Yankee in King Arthur's Court*, and he taught the first animal-drawing class in the world in 1893. His ability throughout his books to see the world through the eyes of an adventurous country lad still gives his drawings a unique appeal today.

Starting a "three-tree house."

The frame of a one-tree house.

Supports for a two-tree house.

This house, when completed, includes a wraparound porch and, partway up, a landing.

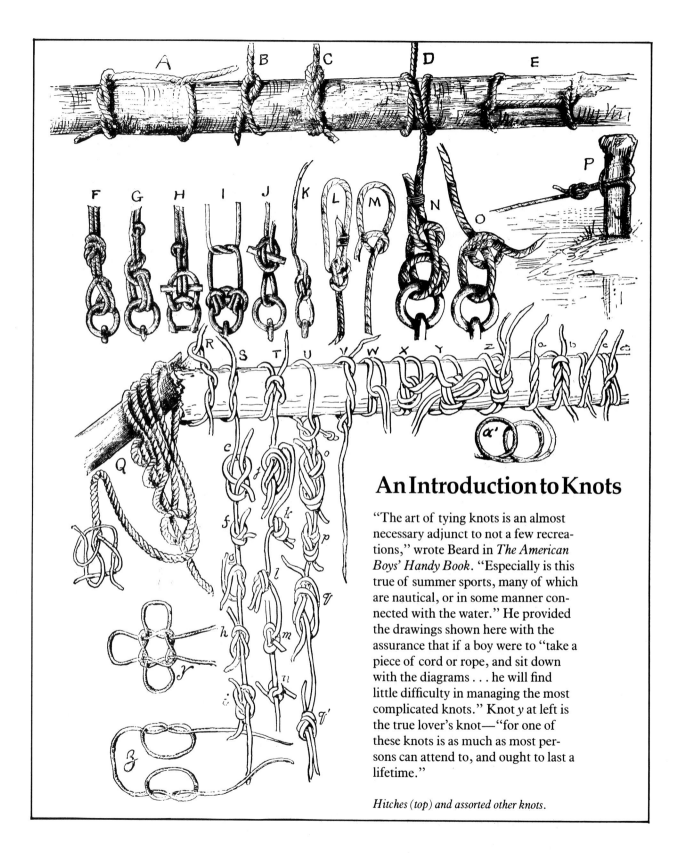

An Introduction to Knots

"The art of tying knots is an almost necessary adjunct to not a few recreations," wrote Beard in *The American Boys' Handy Book*. "Especially is this true of summer sports, many of which are nautical, or in some manner connected with the water." He provided the drawings shown here with the assurance that if a boy were to "take a piece of cord or rope, and sit down with the diagrams . . . he will find little difficulty in managing the most complicated knots." Knot *y* at left is the true lover's knot—"for one of these knots is as much as most persons can attend to, and ought to last a lifetime."

Hitches (top) and assorted other knots.

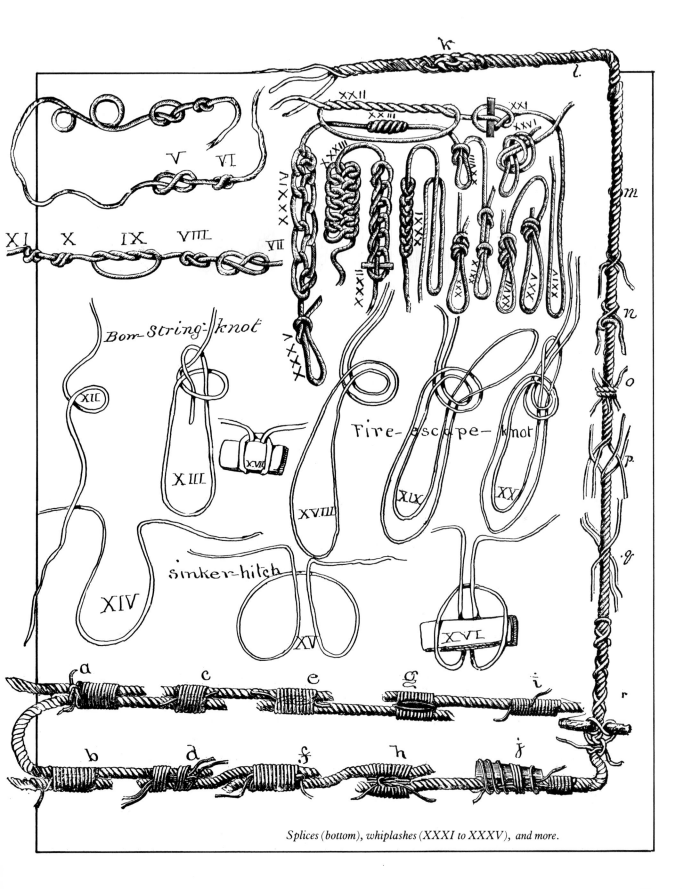

Splices (bottom), whiplashes (XXXI to XXXV), and more.

41

Seton's Woodcraft Sketches

Ernest Thompson Seton— naturalist, wildlife artist, author, and lecturer—became the first Chief Scout in 1910 and immediately penned the first official American handbook, *Boy Scouts of America: A Handbook of Woodcraft, Scouting, and Life-craft*. In it he combined parts of the guide he'd written for his own group, the Woodcraft Indians, and material from Baden-Powell's *Scouting for Boys* (fully acknowledged). The sketch at right of a boy starting a fire is a Baden-Powell original borrowed by Seton; the others are from Seton's own *Woodcraft Manual for Boys*. Totem poles, Seton advised, were important at any camp, "1st, to typify the movement; 2d, to display the Totems of the Tribe; 3rd to serve as a place of notice."

Recommended totem poles. The two at left include bulletin boards.

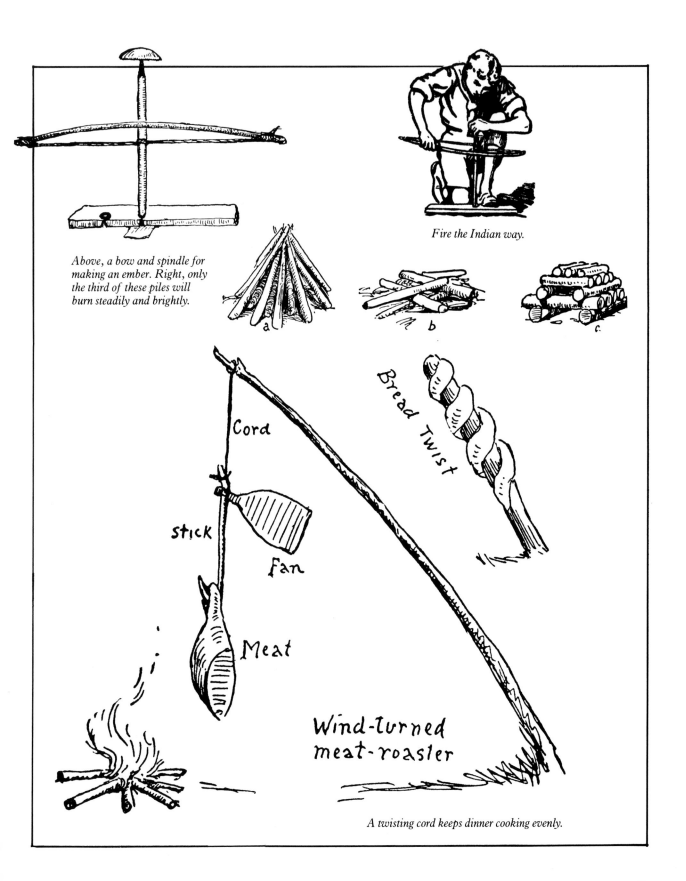

Above, a bow and spindle for making an ember. Right, only the third of these piles will burn steadily and brightly.

Fire the Indian way.

a

b

c

Cord

Stick

Fan

Meat

Bread Twist

Wind-turned meat-roaster

A twisting cord keeps dinner cooking evenly.

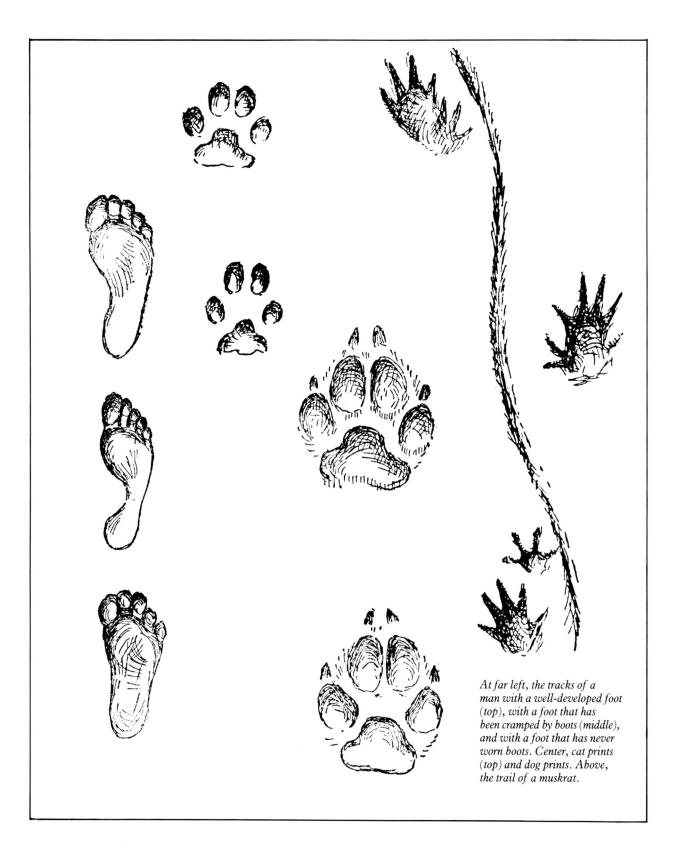

At far left, the tracks of a man with a well-developed foot (top), with a foot that has been cramped by boots (middle), and with a foot that has never worn boots. Center, cat prints (top) and dog prints. Above, the trail of a muskrat.

Tracking With E. T. Seton

Seton's 1910 Boy Scout handbook was so hurriedly put together that the entire text of the chapter on animal tracking, which included the illustrations at left, read: "The first step in tracking or trailing is learning the footmarks of each of the common animals. A number of these are given now. A more elaborate article on the Secrets of the Trail will appear in a subsequent issue." Seton utilized both the experiences of his younger years in the Canadian wilderness and his training as an artist in preparing these drawings. But he admitted that he had never found a fail-safe way to distinguish between dog and wolf tracks; the illustration at right, from *The Book of Woodcraft*, shows the wolf's trail as reflecting a "suspicious, shy creature while the dog-trail is direct, and usually unafraid."

Above, Seton's rendering of the tracks left after an encounter between a dog and a wolf.

Left, a preparatory sketch for the painting shown overleaf, with special attention to paws.

Seton made this oil painting in 1898 and later wrote that his aim had been to convey the way wolves would look chasing behind a speeding sleigh.

2
Birth of the BSA

William Howard Taft, president of the United States and honorary president of the Boy Scouts, greets Scouts during the organization's first years.

IN THE SPRING of 1910, William D. Boyce owned the name "Boy Scouts of America" but he had no Boy Scouts, no organization, and no clear idea of how to get either. He had employed a former clergyman to promote the Scouting idea and organize troops, but the returns were discouraging.

So it was with interest that on May 3 he received three YMCA men who offered to help. The delegation was headed by a tall, athletic-looking, reserved man named Edgar M. Robinson. Before the year was out, Robinson would guide the Boy Scouts of America through its infancy. He was, in effect, the first Chief Scout Executive. When he met Boyce, Robinson was 43 years old and held the title of senior boys' work secretary of the YMCA's International Committee in New York.

Robinson and his colleagues, Dr. L. L. Doggett and J. A. Van Dis, were in a good position to help because the YMCA had 60 years of experi-

ence in working with American youth. It had been operating summer camps for boys since 1885, and by 1910 some 15,000 boys were camping in 400 camps under YMCA auspices. Besides, local Y's were already running Scout troops. They had little trouble persuading Boyce that the YMCA could be the vehicle for getting the BSA off the ground. Boyce pledged to support their efforts with $1,000 a month for an indefinite period. (By the end of 1910, Boyce had contributed $4,000, an amount that was crucial to the young movement's finances. It was no hardship for Boyce; his annual income in those pre-income tax days was estimated at $350,000.)

Armed with Boyce's blessing, Robinson opened a one-room Scout headquarters next to his own office in the YMCA building on East 28th Street in New York. The office force—consisting of a stenographer and John L. Alexander, a YMCA man, as managing secretary—was quickly inundated with mail from men who wanted to start troops.

Something had to be done, and fast. So on June 21, at Robinson's initiative, 25 leaders in various areas of youth and social work gathered to plan a permanent organization. Among them were educators, officers of YMCA's, leaders of the Big Brothers, American Red Cross, Playground and Recreation Association of America, the settlement movement, and Public School Athletic Leagues. The group also included author Lincoln Steffens, Ernest Thompson Seton of the Woodcraft Indians, and Dan Beard of the Boy Pioneers. Colin B. Livingstone, a Washington banker, was elected temporary chairman; he would later serve for 15 years as the BSA's first president. The group appointed a Committee on Organization to devise a permanent structure for the BSA.

Meanwhile, John Alexander was preparing publications as well as coping with the flood of correspondence. The first two pamphlets were issued in July bearing the titles "Boy Scouts of America: Scouting for Boys" and "Hints for Local Councils or Committees." Four other pamphlets were issued later that year. In August the first American Scout handbook, called *Boy Scouts of America: A Handbook of Woodcraft, Scouting, and Life-craft*, came off the press. It was the hasty work of Ernest Thompson Seton, now

named Chief Scout, who combined parts of his own *Birch Bark Roll* and Baden-Powell's *Scouting for Boys*. In the preface, Seton claimed credit for starting Boy Scouting with his Indians, saying that Baden-Powell had incorporated "the principles of the Indians with other ethical features . . . as well as by giving it a partly military organization, and a carefully compiled and fascinating handbook."

Seton did not mention Dan Beard and his Boy Pioneers. Beard was unhappy. He wrote to John Alexander, "The first Mr. Seton knew about real boy scouts was when he called at the editorial rooms of *Recreation* to interview me about my scouts a long time before Baden-Powell's scouts were thought of. . . . Each member of my society is known as a boy scout, although the organization is now called the Boy Pioneers of America."

While Seton's handbook was rolling off the presses, the first Boy Scout camp in the United States was held at Silver Bay on Lake George in upstate New York. Originally it had been planned as a regular YMCA camp with demonstrations by Seton of his Woodcraft Indians methods. But by the time the 2-week camp opened on August 16, all of the camp leaders were involved with the Boy Scouts of America. So it turned into a Scout camp with an Indian flavor.

The campers were 120 boys and 20 adults from YMCA's in the Northeast. In overall charge was William D. Murray, vice-chairman of the YMCA's International Committee, who became a professional Scouter and author of the BSA's first history. Seton was camp chief, with Edgar Robinson as assistant. Each morning the campers had lectures and demonstrations in woodcraft, public health, safety, and other things pertaining to Scouting. The afternoons were free of organized activities; the campers took nature hikes, went swimming, or played ball. The camp marked the beginning of the BSA's advancement program; the campers were invited to test their skills against goals and standards, not against other boys.

Every evening there was a campfire featuring Ernest Thompson Seton. "He usually talked about woodcraft," said William W. Edel, a YMCA camper from Baltimore, Md. "He talked about forest life and trees, finding your way from the way trees grow, and other things connected with woodcraft. He talked a lot about wild animals, and those of us who had read his books about animals were thrilled to hear him tell some of the same stories."

Edel remembered that there were regular discussions in his tepee about whether the American movement should follow British Scouting or lean toward Indian lore. "The leaders of the camp were preaching Boy Scouts, and they convinced us, there's no doubt about that," Edel said. "I came to the camp as a Woodcraft Indian and left as a Boy Scout."

The Boy Scouts of America was rapidly gaining momentum that summer, but it was not alone in the field. By late June, several other groups using the name "Scouts" were trying to recruit boys. The largest and most aggravating to the fledgling BSA was the American Boy Scout movement (later called United States Boy Scouts), headed by newspaper publisher William Randolph Hearst and promoted by his *New York American*. Like most of the competing groups, the American Boy Scouts aimed to train young soldiers; they drilled with real guns, practiced military tactics, and enjoyed sham battles as well as hiking and camping. (But not every American Boy Scout troop was quite so warlike. Orange E. Apple, who later served the BSA for many years as a Scoutmaster, remembered joining an American Boy Scout troop in Chicago which, he said, was much like the troops of the BSA. "It may have been a little more military," he said, "but we hiked and camped and identified nature objects in the forest preserves.")

Other early competitors were the Boy Scouts of the United States, headed by a retired Army colonel named Peter S. Bomus and backed by the National Highway Protective Association, and the National Scouts of America led by William Verbeck, president of a military school in Manlius, N.Y. By the fall of 1910, Bomus and Verbeck had succumbed to Edgar Robinson's gentle persuasion and merged their groups into the BSA. Elsewhere there were efforts to begin organizations with names like the Leatherstocking Scouts and Peace Scouts, but all eventually were absorbed into the growing Boy Scouts of America.

The Committee on Organization that had been appointed in June labored through the summer, and on October 27 the BSA's national Executive Board (then called Board of Managers) was in business. It held legal title to the name "Boy Scouts of America," having received it 2 days before from William D. Boyce.

By the end of 1910, the BSA was unarguably the front-runner in the Scouting movement in this country. Yet the American Boy Scout organization would remain a thorn in the BSA's side for most of the new decade; it lost stature in December, however, when William Randolph Hearst withdrew, charging the organizers with financial irregularities. The BSA had the backing of Baden-Powell, President William Howard Taft had agreed to be honorary president, and the new National Council boasted 35 prominent names, including Admiral George Dewey of Spanish-American War fame, General Leonard Wood, novelist Hamlin Garland, Seton, Beard, Robinson, and Boyce.

Robinson, who had been given the title of executive secretary in November, was invited to stay on permanently, but he declined, preferring to return to his beloved YMCA. His successor was James E. West, a young

Edgar M. Robinson

I REMEMBER . . .

The Scene: *Baltimore, Md., after the first American Scout camp, September 1910*

My group came home to Baltimore enthused over Scouting as no one in the world could be. We were just going to sell it to everybody. From that moment on, until I left Baltimore for college 2 years later, almost every night of the week that first patrol went from school to school, church to church, from lodge to lodge, campsite to playground—wherever we could get a group—and talked and demonstrated Scouting. We won a lot of interest from people, and it was from that beginning, I'm quite sure, that Scouting in Baltimore had its origin.

—*William W. Edel*

lawyer from Washington, D.C., who, over the next 3 decades, would build the Boy Scouts of America into a national institution.

James Edward West, born in Washington in 1876, was orphaned at 6 and sent to the City Orphan Asylum. A year later, when he complained of leg pains, he was punished as a malingerer until a physician diagnosed tuberculosis of the hip and knee. He spent 2 years in a hospital before returning to the orphanage with a permanent limp. During a boyhood spent in that Dickensian setting, James West became the handyman, librarian, laundry operator, night watchman, and keeper of the matron's chickens.

By force of will and foregoing sleep, West finished high school at the age of 19. He joined the orphanage staff and led a campaign of rat extermination and repainting; he also exposed mismanagement by the board of directors. Later he became a bookkeeper in a bicycle shop and read law on the side. In 1901 he earned his law degree from Washington's National University after working his way through school as a YMCA worker and War Department stenographer. Through the influence of President Theodore Roosevelt, with whom he had become friendly, he served on the U.S. Board of Pension Appeals and as an assistant attorney in the Interior Department before entering private law practice in 1906.

Throughout the first decade of the century, West's spare time was given to youth work. He was instrumental in establishing the first juvenile court in Washington, helped set up the city's playground system, and joined with novelist Theodore Dreiser in founding the Child Rescue League, which placed more than 2,000 children in foster homes. With Roosevelt's support, he organized the first White House Conference on the Care of Dependent Children in 1909.

When the leaders of the Boy Scouts of America went looking for an executive, the 34-year-old West was an obvious choice. At first he demurred but finally agreed to serve for 6 months to get the BSA on a solid footing. The 6 months stretched into 32 years.

West was a hard-driving, decisive executive and a demanding boss, infuriating at times, considerate at others. Julian H. Salomon had a ringside seat during West's early years as Chief Scout Executive. He was a part-time office boy in the BSA's national headquarters, with only a glass partition separating his cubicle from West's office. Salomon, who in 1913 earned the 42nd Eagle Scout badge awarded by the BSA and was later a Scout executive, remembered watching West crush anyone or anything he deemed inimical to the interests of the new movement. "He was a real battler, and he could be ruthless," Salomon said. "If anybody used the name Scouts around the United States, he either persuaded them to come into the national organization or he would knock them out by fair means or foul."

In common with others who watched the early development of Scouting in America, Salomon has high praise for West's achievements. "He *made* the organization, no question about it," he said.

As chief executive of a youth group, James E. West longed to appeal to boys as did Seton and Beard. Once, Salomon recalled, "he was going to Brooklyn to visit a troop so he had me in the office teaching him the Tenderfoot knots so he could tie the knots for the kids. He just yearned to make an appeal to kids, but he never could do it."

One of four committees appointed at the first annual meeting of the BSA's National Council was charged with "Americanizing" Baden-Powell's Scout Oath and Law and the advancement requirements for the ranks of Tenderfoot through First Class. The committee labored through the spring of 1911, getting advice from 500 educators.

But in the end, the changes in the Oath and Law were largely the work of the Chief Scout Executive himself. Baden-Powell's Oath had read: "On

my honour I promise that I will do my best to do my duty to God and the King; to help other people at all times; to obey the Scout Law." The obvious change from "the King" to "my country" was made without demur; then, at West's insistence, the phrase was added: "to keep myself physically strong, mentally awake, and morally straight."

Baden-Powell's Scout Law had nine points covering the virtues of trustworthiness, loyalty, helpfulness, friendliness, courtesy, kindness, obedience, cheerfulness, and thrift. For the American Scout Law, the committee changed the wording of each point but retained the meaning. At West's urging, three additional points were added—be brave, clean, and reverent. West was particularly adamant about adding "reverent" because, he said later, "I felt then, as I feel now, that there is nothing more essential in the education of the youth of America than to give them religious instruction."

As one result, religious bodies became Scouting's prime sponsors. The first national religious organization to approve Boy Scouting was the Church of Jesus Christ of Latter-day Saints (Mormon), which adopted Scouting for its youth in 1913.

West brought an executive ability and organizational genius to complement the heart and soul provided by Baden-Powell, Seton, and Beard —talents that were sorely needed to guide the mushrooming growth of the new movement. At the National Council's first annual meeting West reported that 2,000 Scoutmasters had been registered in 1910 and another 2,000 were at work but unregistered. Boy Scouts were not required to register until 1913, but their number at the end of the first year was estimated at 300,000. (In later years, that estimate was reduced to 55,000; the actual

An early troop of blind Scouts marches down a hillside in Kentucky in 1911.

This magazine photo bore the caption, "Every boy can tie a knot, but not seventeen different kinds."

number probably was even lower.) Some 200 local councils or committees had been formed to supervise troops.

To replace Seton's hastily written manual, the first *Handbook for Boys* was published August 31, 1911, after a herculean effort by West and his small staff. It contained the fruits of four specially appointed commissions, giving the new American Scout Oath, Law, and advancement requirements, showing the newly approved uniforms and badges, and offering guidance for organizing patrols and troops. Like today's *Official Boy Scout Handbook*, the *Handbook for Boys* also covered woodcraft and nature lore, camping skills, athletics, health, first aid and lifesaving, and patriotism and citizenship. Sections were contributed by 16 experts in various fields, including Ernest Thompson Seton, the National Association of Audubon Societies, the U.S. Bureau of Entymology, and the Geological Survey.

In Seton's manual, the suggested uniform was the British model. The new *Handbook* showed a uniform that looked like a miniature of the U.S. Army's garb. It called for a khaki campaign hat, a five-button, choke-collar coat, knee breeches, and canvas leggings. The whole outfit cost $4.05.

Early records say that the uniform was the work of a committee, but the prime mover probably was Sigmund Eisner of Red Bank, N.J., whose business was manufacturing uniforms for several of the world's armies and who became the BSA's official uniform and equipment supplier.

The uniform was both a plus and minus for the young movement. Many old Scouts remember that the uniform was a big attraction. Julian Salomon recalled that in the early days "the two things that gave Scouting great impetus and made it very popular were the uniform and Teddy Roosevelt's jingoism. Prior to World War I, I think the preparedness movement had more to do with the growth of Scouting than anything else. All of a sudden everybody wanted to get into a uniform of some kind or other."

But the uniform posed a problem, too, because it hinted at military training. Louis A. Hornbeck remembered joining Troop 23 in Brooklyn in 1912 over his parents' misgivings. "Many people came here from Europe because the male member of the family was threatened with military service," he said. "I suspect that was true of my father, who came here from Denmark. He didn't absolutely discourage me from joining, but there was a concern."

The military flavor that some people saw in Scouting also affected Fielding Chandler, who was growing up in St. Louis in 1912. Chandler, who later became a Scoutmaster, remembered that he did not join as a boy although he attended some troop meetings and hikes. "My parents were not enthusiastic about my becoming a Boy Scout," he said. "It was new and they didn't understand it very well. In those days there was some idea that the boys would graduate from Scouting into the Army."

That perception was understandable, given Baden-Powell's military background, although he did his best to dispel the notion that Scouting was military training; his writings on the movement as "peace Scouting" were picked up in one of the first six pamphlets issued by the Boy Scouts of America. (In later years, Seton claimed that he had been told by Baden-Powell that his original aim had been to prepare English youth for war; the claim was never corroborated by other early Scout leaders.)

Parental concerns about militarism were not entirely unfounded. For one thing, the rival American Boy Scouts were frankly militaristic, and for some years there was considerable confusion in the public mind when the term "Boy Scout" was used. The American Boy Scout organization capitalized on the confusion in its fund-raising, which was one reason West and the other BSA leaders were eager to be rid of it.

For another thing, some of the BSA's own troops did a lot of marching and drilling. Some even used military titles. The first troop in Logansport, Ind., for example, had "corporals" and "sergeants" instead of patrol leaders. Albert Drompp, who joined the Logansport troop in 1912, recalled, "The troop had about 200 boys from all over the county, and our Scoutmaster was a veteran of the Spanish-American War. He wasn't too well acquainted with Scouting, and his activities for us were marching and camping—things he knew something about." When the *Handbook for Boys* arrived in Logansport, troop activities broadened somewhat, but the staples were marching, camping, hiking, swimming, and lifesaving practice.

West issued several pronouncements for the national Executive Board restating the BSA's stance against militarism. Sometimes these followed

Texas's first Boy Scout troop was organized in 1910 at the Dallas YMCA.

OF 'FATHERS' AND 'UNCLES'

For several years after the founding of the Boy Scouts of America, the question of who was first in the Scouting field rankled Ernest Thompson Seton and Daniel Carter Beard. Seton claimed primacy for his Woodcraft Indians, Beard for his Boy Pioneers.

Robert S. S. Baden-Powell stayed aloof, probably because he had the strongest claim. He tried vainly to pour oil on the troubled waters at a banquet in New York in September 1910. Inexplicably, Seton introduced him as the father of Scouting and Baden-Powell replied, "You are mistaken, Mr. Seton, in your remarks to the effect that I am the father of this idea of Scouting for boys. I may say that you, or Dan Beard is the father—there are many fathers. I am only one of the uncles, you may say."

Assessing the claims of Baden-Powell, Seton, and Beard, Edgar M. Robinson wrote later, "They were as different as three men could be in their background experience and ideas. Baden-Powell could not help thinking in military terms; Seton could not help thinking in terms of the Ideal Indian; Beard thought in terms of the 'Knights of the Buckskin' or the old-time frontiersmen who conquered the forest and killed the Indians." All three streams converged in Boy Scouting in America. But, Robinson concluded, Baden-Powell "will stand out, and rightly so, as the real founder of Scouting throughout the world."

As between the claims of Seton and Beard, Seton's contribution was greater. His emphasis on woodcraft and nature lore has been a part of American Scouting from the beginning; to a lesser extent, his esteem for the American Indian lives on, especially in the rituals and symbols of the Order of the Arrow, the BSA's honor campers' society, and in some symbols of Cub Scouting. Dan Beard was the beloved "Uncle Dan" to a generation of Boy Scouts, but little remains of his legacy except the woodcraft skills which his Boy Pioneers shared with Seton's Indians.

accidental shootings of boys who belonged to the American Boy Scouts and drilled with real rifles. West made it clear that no BSA member was authorized to carry firearms; he also frowned on military-type drilling.

By 1915, while World War I was raging in Europe, there was a subtle change in the BSA's position, although not in official policy. America's national preparedness was being debated in the press, and the BSA was accused of being antimilitary because of its insistence that Scouting was not military training. So the Executive Board issued a resolution stating "that the Boy Scout Movement is not anti-military. The Boy Scout Movement neither promotes nor discourages military training, its one concern being the development of character and personal efficiency of adolescent boys."

West and the national Executive Board faced other problems, too. Among them were suspicions by Roman Catholic bishops that Scouting was an arm of the YMCA, and opposition by labor leaders and southern white civic leaders.

The Catholic hierarchy's concern was founded in the fact that the YMCA, a predominantly Protestant organization, furnished most of the leadership for the BSA and was home to many early troops. Their fears were not allayed by a statement in 1910 by Edgar M. Robinson, who wrote: "This national movement is not organically related in any way to the Young Men's Christian Association, but all possible cooperation is being given. . . . "

A few troops were formed in Catholic parishes in the early years, and in 1913 a Catholic was named national field commissioner to promote Scouting in the church, but it was not until 1917 that the hierarchy gave its approval. Cardinal O'Connell of Boston, one of several bishops who endorsed Scouting then, did so with the understanding that "there shall be distinctly Catholic troops under a Catholic Scoutmaster, and that there shall be a Chaplain appointed by the proper ecclesiastical authority for each Catholic troop."

Organized labor leaders feared that Scouts might become strikebreakers because of their reading of Baden-Powell's Scout Law, which was adapted with minor changes in the BSA's first pamphlet. The Scout was called upon to be "loyal to his country, his officers, his parents, and his employers." (The word "employers" was dropped in Seton's handbook and the first *Handbook for Boys*.) In 1911 labor leaders in St. Louis announced that union musicians would not march in a parade if Boy Scouts did. Gradually labor's opposition subsided, and by 1917 the United Mine Workers and the Illinois Federation of Labor endorsed Scouting for the sons of workingmen.

On the matter of race, the BSA followed prevailing laws and customs. Segregation was law in the South, and the question of allowing black boys to become Scouts arose early. In 1911 a leader in the Scout organization in New Orleans, which had not yet affiliated itself with the BSA, wrote to James E. West that he had heard the BSA was admitting blacks. "We cannot keep the white boys of this section in an organization that admits Negroes," he said. "There would be no necessity whatever of the New Orleans Boy Scouts admitting Negro boys into their ranks," West replied. "The Negro interests of the Boy Scout Movement could be handled in the same way you handle the public school question in the South, that is, providing separate schools, separate teachers and administration." A handful of all-black troops had been formed by that time and a few blacks were in white troops in the North, but there would be no national effort to bring black boys into Scouting for 2 decades.

Many enduring features of the Boy Scouts of America were developed in those first hectic years. Sea Scouting, the first program for older boys,

In an advance edition of the 1911 handbook, three badges were announced: Life (top), Star (middle), and Wolf. By publication time, the highest, Wolf, had been replaced by Eagle.

Arthur Eldred, the first Eagle Scout.

The first edition of Boys' Life, *in 1911. The BSA bought it the next year.*

I REMEMBER . . .

The Scene: *Ithaca, N.Y., 1912*

Another fellow and I really started the troop and recruited our friends. I named it the Eagle Patrol of Troop 1. It was really disorganized at that time. Our patrol worked up the whole deal for the first couple of years. Finally we got some students from Cornell University who were interested in youth to act as Scoutmaster and assistant Scoutmasters, and that began an organization of sorts.

As I look back on it, I'm surprised that a small group of 12-year-olds could be so fired up. Of course, it was a new organization and I suppose that had a part in inspiring us to become a part of something that we felt was so basic. It was one of the highlights of my boyhood.

—*LeRoy W. Pritchard*

was born when the BSA was barely a year old. It was started by Arthur A. Carey of Waltham, Mass., who gave the schooner *Pioneer* to Scouts in his area and wrote the first Sea Scout manual.

In 1912 the BSA got into the magazine business, publishing its first issue of *Boys' Life* that July. The magazine, which was destined to grow into the nation's largest publication for youth, had been started in March 1911 by an ambitious 18-year-old Rhode Island Scout named Joseph Lane. Without authorization, Lane had dubbed it the "semi-official publication of the Boy Scouts of America." When the BSA bought it, *Boys' Life* had a monthly circulation of 6,000; the purchase price was $1 per subscriber. A year after taking over *Boys' Life*, the BSA started *Scouting* magazine as a bulletin for Scoutmasters and issued the first edition of the *Handbook for Scoutmasters*.

Meanwhile, the BSA's system of administration was evolving out of the need for promoting Scouting and supervising troops. Local councils began appearing in cities in the late summer of 1910. By 1913 troop committees were growing out of the necessity to provide continuity for troops when Scoutmasters dropped out, and the BSA's regional plan for overseeing local councils was begun with division of the country into eight districts.

Most educators and parents welcomed Scouting as a wholesome influence on boys. Scores of articles and editorials, most of them laudatory, appeared in newspapers and such leading publications as *Literary Digest*, *Outlook*, *Harper's Weekly*, *Good Housekeeping Magazine*, and *Century*.

A mother's view of Scouting was given in the May 1912 issue of *Woman's Home Companion*. In an unsigned article reviewing the *Handbook for Boys*, the author said that much of it was "claptrap, a kind of playing and make-believe." But, she added, "there are pages, too, that glowed with the light

Early Scouts examine a wooden airplane of their own construction. They are wearing one of the first official uniforms, with jodhpurs, tight collars, and flat-brimmed hats.

In this Rockwell drawing, campers kid a new troop member who made the mistake of wearing pajamas.

An early illustration by Norman Rockwell—for The Boy Scout's Hike Book, *published in 1913.*

from a boy's own world. Also, there was the page of Scout Laws, reading which, something in me got to its feet and saluted as a cadet salutes a superior officer. . . . I had hoped my boy would be all these things, and had so admonished him. But these are Scout Laws, mind you, not advice and admonition, not hopes backed by maternal pleadings and fears, but laws, self-imposed when the Scout takes his oath. . . . That settled it. If the Scout movement stood for these things and inspired and exacted them, I was with it heart and soul.''

Her enthusiasm for the aims of Scouting reflected growing acceptance by Americans both young and old. Boys were flocking to sign up, usually with parental encouragement. Nearly three-quarters of a century later, some remembered their great adventure.

Lt. Gen. Daniel B. Strickler (Ret.), member of Troop 1, Columbia, Pa., in 1910:

"Scouting got to be very important to us. As troops developed around the county, Scouting was highly regarded—and used. The Boy Scouts helped a lot around the community. It made men of them. When we had our first camp, the kids were 10, 11, 12, 13 years old, and some of them had a hard time adjusting to the rigors of that camp. They got homesick.''

Frederic J. Closser, who joined Troop 1, Ontario, N.Y., in 1912:

"Our first activity was a camping trip to Lake Ontario north of our village. We walked, and a farm wagon carried our duffel, which consisted mostly of tarpaulins and horse blankets. A horse blanket in those days was a *horse* blanket, and it smelled like it. We had a large cauldron like those used in butchering farm animals, and we did all our cooking in that, so we had soup or stew every day.''

Otis H. Chidester, Boys' Brigade member in Susquehanna, Pa., in 1912:

"Susquehanna was a division point on the Erie Railroad. There was a Railroad YMCA there, and a Y secretary had started a Boys' Brigade several years before. I joined that in July 1912. That September when school started, our parents had a meeting at the YMCA, and they decided they'd like to have the Boys' Brigade changed over to Scouting. So that was how we went into Scouting.''

Ivo V. Pennington, member of Nebraska's first troop, Troop 1 of Wauneta, said that in 1912:

"There wasn't any place to meet in town, so they went out on the edge of town and dug a cave in the side of a small valley and roofed it over with logs and then brush and dirt. That was the troop meeting place.''

Rea E. Nunnallee, member of Troop 1, Van Alstyne, Tex., 1913:

"There were no paved streets here, and the cars and wagons carried the black mud around here up on the sidewalks. You've never been stuck in mud until you've been stuck in *this* black mud. So one of our projects was to see that the sidewalks from here to the school building were kept clean.''

For thousands of boys, especially in isolated small towns, Boy Scouting was thrilling because it offered them a chance to test their mettle and be recognized for it. By the end of 1914, nearly 5 years after the birth of the Boy Scouts of America, 107,000 boys and 25,800 men were registered. Boy Scouts could be seen in every large city and most small towns across America. Even faster growth was ahead.

Saluting the Colors
of Scouting

A Scout leader teaches 10-year-old Webelos Scouts about proper care of the flag.

The Eagle badge (above) has been earned by some boys who grew up to become famous, but Gerald Ford (near right) was the first to become President. He earned it in 1927, at age 14, and has remained active in Scouting ever since.

Above All, the Eagle

Some 25,000 American boys earn the Eagle badge every year. In 1982, 13-year-old Alexander Holsinger, of Normal, Ill., became the one millionth Eagle Scout, and his landmark achievement was greeted with a flurry of national media attention and a phone call from the President. Holsinger's deeds on the home front —including the restoration of an over-grown Civil War cemetery—had been more commendable than spectacular, but he handled the publicity coolly. "I love Scouting," Alex said, at his nationwide press conference. "It has offered me the fun of outdoor activities, the challenge of leadership, and the chance to build self-confidence through skills that will last me a lifetime." He rose to the occasion as an Eagle should.

Upon attaining the rank of Eagle, every Scout is given a red, white, and blue embroi-dered patch (right), as well as the silver eagle on the opposite page.

Holsinger's mother pins on the one millionth Eagle.

Above, a land-surveying exhibit.

Above, orienteering; below, the beekeeping merit-badge display.

Awards for Achievement

The merit badge program has helped Scouts set and attain goals for themselves throughout Scouting's history. A Scout is urged not to pitch himself against rivals but to select interest areas for his own growth. The BSA has revised the more than 100 badge categories constantly over the years—Beef Production was replaced by Animal Science in 1978, and Pigeon Raising was dropped altogether in 1980. Along with merit badges, 12 basic skill awards help Scouts move up through the ranks to Eagle. Scout John Huneke sought the Citizenship in the Community merit badge as he lay in a New York hospital in 1980, stricken with cancer and eager to become an Eagle. He struggled to organize a blood drive to earn the badge—as well as to aid the hospital and improve his own condition. Thanks to the help of school friends, the drive succeeded, the badge was earned, and the Eagle was awarded 2 weeks before John's death.

Scouts waited in lines to get into booths at Merit Badge Midway at the 1981 national jamboree. In the booths, several of which are shown on this page, they could earn points toward badges.

Carol Wigley, opposite, displays eight medals she won at the 1980 Explorer Olympics, in Colorado.

John Godsey, a merit badge counselor in Birmingham, Ala., advises a Scout on woodcarving.

Working Toward a Badge

"The Scouts have to truly earn the merit badges I teach. Anybody that gets something for nothing, really gets nothing. He loses." So says John Schoppert of Alabama, one of thousands of adult counselors who have helped Scouts master valuable skills to qualify for merit badges. The BSA stresses in its Advancement Guidelines that the ideal relation between a Scout and his merit badge counselor is "a one-on-one arrangement in which the boy is not only judged on his performance of the requirements, but receives maximum benefit from the knowledge, skill, character, and personal interest of his counselor." As a result, each badge brings with it the memory of many an evening spent with an exacting but helpful counselor.

At left, a member of a Naples, Florida, troop, on an outing to the Everglades, learns how easily one can, if prepared, live off the land. His day's experience may help him earn a Wilderness Survival Merit Badge. An understanding of man's relationship to the land is also honored by the Conservation Skill Award (above), one of twelve belt loops that whole troops can work toward together.

The Webelos on these pages belong to Pack 22 in Oak Park, Ill. Here, they carry a log for use in lashing practice.

Former Webelos Scout John Brow shows off his graduation certificate just after the ceremony in which he has become a Boy Scout.

Stepping Up in Rank

The colorful regalia of Scouting makes every advancement from one level to the next a celebrated and clearly recorded event. Remarks one Cubmaster, "If you provide this type of recognition . . . from the time they're 8 years old through the time when they're teenagers, they'll keep driving." Webelos —10-year-old boys—are promoted out of the child-oriented activities of Cub Scouts and prepared for the greater challenges that face Boy Scouts. Wearing their distinctive neckerchiefs and shoulder patches, they earn awards toward the night when they may cross a ceremonial bridge and officially become Boy Scouts.

Webelos Scouts learn to make an apple pie. Whereas Cub Scout leadership is traditionally provided by women, Webelos encounter more male leaders.

73

A Scout Is Reverent

Although the Boy Scouts have always stressed the importance of every person's religious duty, there were no awards for special service to God until 1939, when the BSA and the Roman Catholic Church established the first religious emblem program. Since then, many other Christian denominations—as well as Jewish, Buddhist, and Moslem religious groups—have initiated similar programs. They are conferred by religious leaders, not the BSA, and each faith has its own requirements. Nearly half of all Scouting units in the United States are chartered to religious bodies, and these emblems, worn on the chest, reflect the BSA's law of duty to God.

Scouts at an open-air service join together in ecumenical worship. Such services have become regular parts of council camporees and national and international jamborees.

Religious Emblems

The Salvation Army

Church of Jesus Christ of the Latter-day Saints

Unitarian-Universalist

General Protestant

Buddhist

Eastern-Rite Catholic

Roman Catholic

Jewish

Roman Catholic

Islamic

Eastern Orthodox

Reorganized Latter-Day Saints

An Order of Distinction

Each year Scouts can honor especially worthy members of their troop by electing them to the Order of the Arrow, also known as the Brotherhood of Cheerful Service. The purpose of the Order is to promote Scout camping, and the honor is a way of recognizing those BSA campers who best exemplify the Scout Oath and Law in their daily lives. Nobody can apply to join the Order—selection is entirely up to the members of the troop—and when a Scout is chosen, he knows it's a clear sign that he is held in the highest esteem by his fellow campers.

A ceremony is held to induct new members of the Order of the Arrow at Crow Wing Scout Reservation in Minnesota.

Top row, left to right: Henry Fonda, Gerald Ford, Willis Reed, Mark Spitz; middle: Hank Aaron, Richard Roundtree; James Stewart; bottom: James Lovell, Rich Little, David Hartman.

Adult Heroes of Scouting

In 1926, the BSA began to honor American adults who, either through the Scouts or independently, had provided noteworthy service to the nation's youth. The Silver Beaver (local), Silver Antelope (regional), and Silver Buffalo (national) awards were created, and among the winners of the Silver Buffalo (right), the highest award in Scouting, have been Charles Lindbergh, Franklin D. Roosevelt, Norman Rockwell, Walt Disney, and Ronald Reagan. At left are 10 very familiar former Scouts who participated in a Scouting ad campaign in the early 1980's.

John Glenn, astronaut, Marine Corps colonel, Scouter, and later United States Senator, receives a Silver Buffalo in 1965.

3
Scouting Becomes a Household Word

It is fine to have the boys of the country organized for the purposes the Boy Scouts represent, and whenever I see a group of them I am proud of their manliness, and feel cheered by the knowledge of what their organization represents.

—President Woodrow Wilson, 1915

A BOY SCOUT OF TODAY who got caught in a 1915 time warp would feel right at home. The Scout uniforms would look quaint to him, of course, and he might be taken aback by the primitive camping equipment—bedrolls instead of sleeping bags, pup tents (if the troop had tents at all), and cooking utensils borrowed from mom's kitchen.

But a typical troop meeting would hold few surprises for the modern Scout. He would see a flag ceremony, recitation of the familiar Scout Oath and Law, instruction in knot-tying, first aid, or some other advancement requirement, a game of Capture the Flag or Steal the Bacon, patrol meetings, and a closing ceremony. The one alien element would be marching or close-order drill, which in most troops was regarded more as an aid to discipline than as a military exercise.

The advancement tests were different in many respects (notably learning four knots for Tenderfoot, signaling for Second Class, and 14-mile hike for First Class), and there was less emphasis on advancing in rank.

New Jersey Scouts take to the streets with war-bond posters, doing their part to assist the national drive.

Frank Leyendecker's famous poster helped stir the nation to buy war bonds.

Ernest Thompson Seton

Few Scouts progressed into the three highest ranks; the progression then was from Life to Star to Eagle, instead of today's Star, Life, Eagle. More than 50 merit badges were offered, including badges for such vocational and hobby fields as Architecture, Art, Automobiling, Aviation, Blacksmithing, Business, Carpentry, Electricity, Invention, Machinery, Mining, Photography, Plumbing, and Sculpture.

The program was not what Ernest Thompson Seton had had in mind when he became Chief Scout in 1910. The Chief Scout's position was largely ceremonial, with no executive responsibilities, but Seton had worked hard and lent his considerable prestige to the new movement. He had viewed Scouting as an extension of his Woodcraft Indians, with modifications by Baden-Powell, and he disdained "city Scouting" and "knot-tying in church basements." However, his ideas repeatedly clashed with those of his temperamental opposite, James E. West, and Seton lost virtually every battle in the National Council.

The final break occurred late in 1915. Calling a press conference on December 5, Seton announced that he had resigned as Chief Scout in February and complained that the National Council had failed to accept his resignation and was still using his name. Summing up his view of Scouting, Seton said, "Seton started it; Baden-Powell boomed it; West killed it." He described West as "a man of great executive ability, but without knowledge of the activities of boys; who has no point of contact with boys, and who, I might almost say, has never seen the blue sky in his life."

West and the National Council replied in kind, stating that there was no resignation to accept because the Council had quietly failed to reelect Seton as Chief Scout. The reason, West said, was that Seton was not an American citizen and would not "make a definite promise" that he would be naturalized. The Chief Scout Executive also said that Seton had made repeated objections to the section on patriotism in the 1911 *Handbook for Boys* and had "contended that the Boy Scouts of America should not undertake to have boys pledge allegiance to their country, but should leave them free to support our country when they thought it was right and to damn it when they thought it was wrong." Seton, West charged, "was in harmony with the views of anarchists and radical socialists."

After this acrimonious exchange, Seton dropped from Scouting's sight and devoted himself to the Woodcraft League of America, the successor to his Woodcraft Indians. (In 1926 the breach was patched over when Seton was one of the first 22 recipients of the Silver Buffalo award for outstanding service to youth. Seton's award was the seventh—not first or second as he believed was his due—and he did not attend the presentation. Incidentally, at his death on October 23, 1946, in Santa Fe, N.M., Seton was an American citizen.) The departure of Seton caused no tremors at Scouting's grass roots because the program was already firmly entrenched on Baden-Powell's model.

More than half of the 7,375 troops registered at the end of 1915 were sponsored by religious institutions, including 40 in synagogues. The Methodists led the way with 1,171 troops. Nearly half the Scoutmasters were clergymen or businessmen.

Clergymen, especially, realized the appeal of Scouting to boys and its value as a church youth program. The Reverend Herman A. Meyer, who began a 43-year career as a Scout leader in Staten Island, N.Y., in 1916, remembered, "I found no decent youth program at Emmanuel Lutheran when I came there, so we took the Boy Scout program and used that. I followed the *Handbook for Boys*. I had to learn it myself, and I just stayed a little ahead of the boys in the book."

Similarly, the Reverend John D. Clinton formed the first troop in South Walpole, Mass., after hearing lectures about Scouting while he was a theological student at Boston University. And in Plainfield, Conn., the pastor of the First Congregational Church went all out when he formed a troop in 1915 for his congregation's youth. A charter member, Alfred Taylor, Sr., recalled, "There were quite a few of us, and we were running wild, you might say. The church built a small clubhouse for us in back of the parsonage and they outfitted it very well; they put in trapeze and rings, and they even put a pool table on the second floor."

These early church-sponsored troops accepted boys who were not members of the congregation, but occasionally religion was a barrier. Harry Weiner, a young Jewish immigrant from Russia, was growing up in Lynn, Mass., around 1915 when his pal, another Jewish lad, joined a troop in a church. "I got all het up to join, too, but my mother wouldn't hear of my going into a church," he remembered. "Luckily, in 1916 they started a troop at the Boys' Club." He joined that troop and later led a troop in a Hebrew school in Lynn, one of the few Jewish-sponsored troops in that era. "For 20-odd years I was the only Jewish Scoutmaster in the area," Weiner said.

Ernest Thompson Seton (right) instructs a Scout leader at his Silver Bay Camp in 1912.

There was little formal training for Scoutmasters. Most operated their troops with guidance only from the Scout and Scoutmaster's manuals. As a result, there were differing emphases in troop activities. Nearly all the early troops hiked and camped, some as often as weekly. A few stressed marching and drilling; others specialized in astronomy, radio, or whatever skill or hobby the leader might have.

Some were decidedly odd. The Boys' Club troop in Lynn, for example, featured parliamentary procedure. "The Scoutmaster, who was superintendent of the Boys' Club, didn't have much of a Scouting background, but I think he was a lodge man," Harry Weiner said. "At troop meetings, we had a regular ceremonial opening, with a series of questions and answers, and most of our meetings were parliamentary. At every meeting one boy would get up and propose a bean supper, and then we'd spend a good part of the meeting discussing whether we should or shouldn't have it." Fortunately, the Scoutmaster was astute enough to find an assistant who could teach Scout skills, too, or the troop might have evolved into a debating society.

As is still true today, the chief appeal of Scouting was not the troop meetings but the chance to get outdoors. Overnight hikes were at least monthly events in most troops. The Scouts would make bedrolls of their groundcloths, blankets, change of underwear and personal gear, sling it across their shoulders and tie it at the hip, and take off. Hikes of from 7 to 10 miles to a secluded grove or riverbank were common. Tents and other heavy gear were hauled in horse-drawn wagons or in two-wheeled trek carts made—and pulled—by Scouts. City troops preceded their hikes with an hour or two of travel on trolleys, subways, or interurban railways to get to the fringes of the metropolis.

Local councils were rapidly acquiring or leasing camp properties. The first council camp was Owasippe, which was opened in southern Michigan for the Scouts of Chicago in 1912. It was followed in short order by camps for the Scouts of Washington, Philadelphia, and other cities. By 1914 it was estimated that 50,000 Scouts—nearly half the membership—had spent time in camps, most of them in council camps.

But thousands of troops still found their own campsites and camped by themselves on an acre or two of farmland or public lands. Some troops couldn't get enough of camping. For example, Troop 2 of Dover, Ohio, spent virtually all summer—from the week after school let out until the week before it reopened—on the banks of a creek 4 miles from Dover. Paul P. Turbey remembered, "When we needed groceries, we sent two kids down the railroad track to Dover and they carried back the food in a washbasket." Parents visited the Scouts in the evenings, and several adults were with the troop all summer.

The rapid growth of camping is remarkable when one remembers that in the pre–World War I era, few Scoutmasters had any camping experience before taking over troops. Recognizing the need for safety, health, and program standards for Scout camps, the National Council established the Camping Department in 1917.

By that time, an important element of today's Scout camping was slowly evolving. It was the Order of the Arrow, an honor society of campers that perpetuated Seton's idealization of the American Indian. The Order was born in the summer of 1915 in the Philadelphia Council's new camp on Treasure Island in the Delaware River north of Trenton, N.J.

The founders were camp director E. Urner Goodman and his assistant, Carroll A. Edson. Seeking to establish a camp tradition that would carry on from year to year, Edson recalled having heard Seton tell of his success with Indian ceremonies at Woodcraft Indian camps. Edson suggested that the lore of the Lenni Lenape tribe of the Delaware Indians who had formerly inhabited the campsite offered an ideal vehicle.

So on July 16, 1915, the first 25 members of the Order of the Arrow were inducted in solemn Indian-style ceremonies at Treasure Island. By 1918 lodges of the Order had been founded at other Scout camps in New Jersey, Maryland, New York, and Illinois, but it was not until 1921 that it became a national organization. The following year the Order became an official experimental program of the Boy Scouts of America and began growing into the 145,000-member organization it is today with its colorful Indian dance teams and its tradition of service to Scout camps and campers.

Not all Boy Scouts of those days had to be content with recreations of Indian life and lore. Thomas May, who became a Scout about 1913 in Dustin, Okla., in the heart of the old Indian territory, remembered that his Scoutmaster was a full-blooded Creek. Half the boys in the troop were Indian, half whites. "We made things like bows and arrows that were common to Indians, and we boys went to the stomp dances the Indians held," he said. "The Indian boys and white boys got along fine," May added.

The American Indian motif was also continued by the Lone Scouts of America, which was founded as a separate organization in 1915 by William D. Boyce, the original incorporator of the Boy Scouts of America. Boyce had spent much of his time traveling during the first years of the BSA and had not been a leader in its early growth and trials.

He started the Lone Scouts of America for farm boys and lads in isolated villages who had no chance to join a troop, including the 20,000-odd young salesmen of his publications. Hundreds of city boys also joined; some were Boy Scouts and Lone Scouts simultaneously.

Like Boy Scouting, Lone Scouting was an English import, having begun there in 1913. The Lone Scouts of America, however, had a distinctly American flavor, typified by their Indian symbols and titles. Boyce was Chief Totem, although he had little to do with development of the Lone Scout program and rarely was seen by Lone Scouts. To them, he was merely an impressive presence at the Chicago headquarters.

The identifying symbol of Lone Scouting was the figure of a dignified Indian giving the sign of peace with arms upraised and palms down. The Indian appeared on the cover of early issues of the weekly *Lone Scout* magazine, the main vehicle for communication between the boys and headquarters. *Lone Scout* also financed the organization; in the beginning, the penny cost of each issue was the only membership fee. In 1920 the magazine began monthly publication and cost 10 cents.

Boyce hired F. Allen Morgan, who was Scoutmaster of Chicago's largest troop, to edit *Lone Scout* and develop the tests by which Lone Scouts earned ranks (called degrees) by doing Scoutcraft on their own and sending reports to headquarters. Morgan also designed the badges and ghostwrote articles for Chief Totem Boyce.

Morgan's son, Warren F. Morgan, who was an early Eagle Scout and became Lone Scout No. 1, said his father used his experience as Scoutmaster and his admiration for the writings of Dan Beard and Ernest Thompson Seton in writing the degree tests. (The term "degree" evidently was borrowed from the Masons; F. Allen Morgan was an ardent Mason.)

Warren Morgan remembered, "He used me as a guinea pig to try out these tests, and looking back on it now, I feel that it was a little unfair because I was a lot more advanced than most of the boys who were going to tackle these things."

Within a couple of years of its founding, the Lone Scouts of America had tens of thousands of members. In towns where several boys belonged, they formed tribes (the equivalent of patrols) and Scouted together. Many of them were contributors to *Lone Scout* magazine. In the magazine's heyday, about two-thirds of the articles and drawings were contributed by boys, many of whom earned Lone Scouting's Gold Quill award and went on to become newspapermen, writers, and poets. Some tribes had their own little papers to supplement *Lone Scout*.

The early Lone Scouts developed an extraordinary esprit de corps considering that communication among them was mainly through correspondence and publications. Pen pal clubs called mail tribes flourished, and the arrival of *Lone Scout* magazine was a treasured moment in the lives of Lone Scouts. "It definitely was the magazine that brought us together," said Frederick E. Munich, an early Lone Scout. Warren Morgan agreed. "Part of it," he said, "was this feeling of participation rather than just being a reader, and part of it was constant correspondence; boys made friends all over the country that way."

Lone Scouts' loyalty to each other lived on after the LSA was absorbed by the Boy Scouts of America in 1924. Even today two alumni associations, the Elbeetian Legion founded by Charles J. Merlin and the Lone Indian Fellowship, continue the tradition. The Lone Scouting spirit is perpetuated through the pages of their publications, *The Elbeetee* and *Lone Indian*. Regular reunions are held, and a museum of Lone Scouting is maintained at the John J. Barnhardt Scout Camp in New London, N.C.

When Boyce agreed to merge his Lone Scouts of America with the BSA, it was estimated that 45,000 Lone Scouts were active. A total of 523,470 had been members during the 10-year life of the LSA. A Lone Scout division was established at the BSA's national office, supplanting the Pioneer Division, which had been started by the BSA in 1916 to serve rural boys. Pioneers had followed the regular Boy Scout advancement program, with an adult—usually a teacher, clergyman, or the boy's employer—as guide and test examiner. Like the Lone Scouts, Pioneers were urged to form troops if possible, even if they could meet only once a month. The Pioneer program was much less successful than Lone Scouting; the number of registered Pioneers never exceeded 2,000.

For several years after the merger, Lone Scouts could continue to earn their own degrees. Vestiges of the LSA program continued into the

A two-story-tall Scout dramatizes a 1915 fund drive in New York.

*President Woodrow Wilson (left) inspects
Scouts on the eve of World War I.*

mid-1930's when Lone Scouting was fully integrated into Boy Scouting. Lone Scouting (and Lone Cub Scouting) continue today as programs of the Boy Scouts of America, although there are only a few hundred members around the United States.

By the spring of 1916 membership in the BSA was approaching 200,000, and Congress recognized the movement's value and growing strength by granting it a federal charter on June 15. The charter gave formal protection to the name, insignia, and terminology of the young organization. Two weeks earlier, Congress had approved the Boy Scout uniform in the National Defense Act. The act prohibited the unauthorized wearing of uniforms similar to those of the U.S. military, but exempted the Boy Scouts, despite the similarity of the Boy Scout uniform to the Army's. To differentiate Scouts and Scout leaders from soldiers, the Scout pin was worn on the campaign hat.

Armed with the federal charter, the Boy Scouts of America had the muscle to put an end to its only competitor, the militaristic United States

Boy Scout movement. The BSA filed suit against the U.S. Boy Scouts (originally American Boy Scouts), seeking an injunction against their use of the terms "Boy Scout," "Scout," and "Scouting" and all fund-raising using those terms. As always, the wheels of justice ground slowly, and it was not until 1918 that the injunction was granted, effectively ending the United States Boy Scout organization. At its end, the U.S. Boy Scouts claimed a membership of 200,000; the real figure probably was about 3,000.

Finally, the Boy Scouts of America was unchallenged in the field.

It was not, however, the demise of the U.S. Boy Scouts that made the Boy Scouts of America the preeminent youth movement in the United States. The BSA did that itself by prodigies of home-front service during World War I.

The war had started in August 1914, pitting Germany, Austria-Hungary and Turkey against France, Great Britain, Russia, Belgium, and later, Italy. The United States was confident that it could remain aloof from the European conflict, and Woodrow Wilson was reelected President in 1916 with the slogan, "He kept us out of war."

Not for long, though. Germany began unrestricted submarine warfare and sank several U.S. merchant ships; on April 6, 1917, the United States declared war on Germany.

The declaration was the signal for a burst of patriotic fervor that swept over most Americans, including Boy Scouts. The following day the BSA's national Executive Board committed Scouts to the war effort. The Board urged every Scout to plant a garden under the slogan, "Every Scout to feed a soldier"; pledged aid to the American Red Cross in meeting its wartime responsibilities; and promised cooperation with the Navy by organizing a Scout coastal patrol to watch for enemy ships.

At the outbreak of the war, the Boy Scouts of America was the largest uniformed body in the country with 268,000 men and boys (although not every troop had uniforms, and not every Scout had full regalia). The U.S. Army had about 200,000 men and was woefully unprepared for war. A draft was immediately instituted, and by the end of the war in 1918, 4.8 million Americans were under arms.

The BSA's most significant service was in the sale of Liberty Loan bonds issued by the Treasury to finance the war effort. Five Liberty Loan drives were held, the last coming after the armistice was signed on November 11, 1918, and in each case the Boy Scouts were called upon to follow up the regular canvass by adult volunteer salesmen. Despite the handicap of being gleaners after the reapers, Scouts sold a total of 2,238,308 bonds worth $355 million.

Scouts all over the country went door to door to homes, businesses, and industries. Some troops set up booths or trek carts plastered with Liberty Loan posters and got pledges from passersby. Boy Scouts also sold the Treasury's War Savings Stamps and accounted for $3 million worth of sales.

Nearly 70,000 Scouts earned Treasury Department medals for selling bonds to at least 10 people; thousands won extra bars on their medals for additional sales of bonds and stamps. Among the champion salesmen was Joseph D. Wooding of Troop 1, Garretsford (now Drexel Hill), Pa. His

Wartime Scouts collect peach pits for use in gas-mask respirators.

Liberty Loan bond sales topped $150,000, compared to a nationwide average of about $900 per Scout. Wooding's success was due less to salesmanship than to happenstance. He had his own mail service, carrying mail twice a day 6 days a week from the post office to the homes of the affluent. During the Liberty Loan campaigns, Wooding followed up mail deliveries with a pitch for the bonds. He remembered, "I had one customer who was a very wealthy man and he gave me a check for $50,000. Here I am, a 14-year-old kid with a check for $50,000 in my pocket. I thought I was John D. Rockefeller."

Naturally, Wooding collected all the Treasury Department medals. So did C. Brower Woodward, who sold 40 bonds in Newark, N.J., and recalled that he was given a German Army helmet after the war for his prowess as a bond salesman.

Thousands of troops also took part in other home-front campaigns. Many Scouts from the World War I era remember collecting peach pits and nut hulls, which were burned to make charcoal for gas mask filters. All told, more than 100 railroad carloads were gathered by Scouts. Others remember making a census of standing black walnut trees, whose wood was prized for gunstocks and airplane propellers. Boy Scouts went from farm to farm, woodlot to woodlot, to locate the valuable tree. By war's end they had reported the location of 21 million board feet, enough to fill 5,200 railroad cars.

The earliest of the BSA's wartime efforts—gardening—was the least successful, perhaps because so many Scouts were city boys who had no place for a garden. Even so, 12,000 Scout farms and gardens were planted during the two growing seasons of America's participation in World War I.

Boy Scouts who lived along the Atlantic coast were called upon to report ship movements to Naval authorities. In some inland towns they also aided local authorities who feared sabotage. In Ramsey, N.J., for instance, Boy Scouts joined the home guard in patrolling the town's reservoir against the possibility of sabotage. "We were supposed to see that no one came up and put poison in it," Newton Woodruff of Troop 31 recalled. "Nobody ever showed up that I remember."

Scouts also served as dispatch bearers for government agencies and delivered 30 million pamphlets on the war effort. In addition, Scouts aided the Red Cross, the United War Work Committee, and other groups.

In a few communities, Scout leaders had their own agenda for war service. E. W. Armistead, who was a Scout in Memphis, Tenn., remembered that a retired cavalry officer selected some older Scouts and began training them to defend the city against possible attack by the Germans. (A few years earlier, a German sub had come up the Mississippi and visited Memphis.) "We started out drilling with the old Springfield rifles, and then Woodrow Wilson said we'd have to use wooden rifles," Armistead said. "That kind of put a damper on it. We didn't like it because they called us wooden soldiers." So the select troop became an emergency service corps, training for crowd control and disaster work.

In the twin cities of Texarkana on the border of Texas and Arkansas, Troop 1 drilled with wooden rifles, too. "There was no advertisement that we were doing it but it wasn't a secret, either," Wilbur Smith recalled. "Our Scoutmaster, Mr. Riley, found himself having to try to convince our parents that he wasn't training their boys to be soldiers, and I don't want you to think he was trying to make an army out of us."

Most troops did some marching and close-order drill during the war, although few carried even dummy guns. Frequently Scout troops were called out to parade—always on Memorial Day when veterans of the Civil and Spanish-American wars joined the doughboys of World War I in commemorating the war dead.

In Birmingham, Ala., Claude Thompson remembered, "Hardly a week went by that we weren't called out to march in a parade or help with traffic control for one." Whenever a train came through Birmingham with a contingent of soldiers, and immediately after the war when the troops were being demobilized, a parade would be held. "Sometimes we also helped

With an ax for a hammer, a Scout nails up a Liberty Bond poster in 1917.

Soon after America's entry into the war in 1917, these Scouts were photographed running down New York's Fifth Avenue for a patriotic rally and bond sale.

Treasury Secretary William McAdoo stands before six Scouts receiving special medals for their achievements in the war bond drives.

invalid soldiers who needed personal escorts," Thompson said. "We would be assigned to help those in wheelchairs and on crutches."

Nationwide Good Turns during World War I focused the public's attention on Boy Scouts but they were not the first major services undertaken by the Boy Scouts of America. As early as 1912, Boy Scouts had distributed literature and posters to promote a "Safe and Sane Fourth of July."

The following year Scouts from several northeastern states formed an escort, first aid and traffic control service at a reunion of more than 5,000 Union and Confederate soldiers marking the 50th anniversary of the Civil War's Battle of Gettysburg. That same year, when Ohio and Indiana were hit by disastrous floods, thousands of Boy Scouts were called out to aid the Red Cross by distributing food and clothing, serving as aides and messengers for local authorities, and manning soup kitchens. In later years Scouts did yeoman service following many other natural disasters.

In some towns, Boy Scouts formed a permanent emergency force. In Naugatuck, Conn., whenever a child was missing or elderly people needed help, the fire whistle sounded a special call—three short blasts four times. Cecil F. Matson, a Scout in Naugatuck's Troop 2, remembered, "When we heard that call, all the Scouts in town ran to the firehouse immediately." The call came four or five times a year, he said, "and I remember being called out a number of times in the middle of the night."

I REMEMBER . . .

The Scene: *Muscatine, Iowa, in 1918*

The daughter of one of the wealthy lumbermen around here was quite active in the Daughters of the American Revolution. She called up my uncle, who was a Scouter in Troop 2, one day and said, "The DAR is going to have a convention here and we want to have a parade and have all the Scouts march in it." My uncle said, "Well, we can march but we don't have more than one or two uniforms in the whole troop."

"Well," she said, "I took care of that. You go down to the clothing store. They've got orders to measure every boy for a uniform. They'll be ready in time for that parade."

Boy, were we ever proud kids! Brand new uniforms for all of us!
                                                              —*Howard Carl*

Membership in the Boy Scouts of America soared by more than 60 percent during the war as boys rushed to get into uniform and have a part in the fight against the Kaiser. At the end of 1918, 2 months after the armistice, the BSA had 419,000 registered members. Before the war Boy Scouts had been a visible presence in big cities and many small towns. At war's end, Scouting was a household word.

In 1919, with many former doughboys taking up or resuming positions as Scoutmasters, the movement had promising leadership at the local level. Membership as the BSA neared its tenth anniversary was 468,000 and was still growing briskly, although less rapidly than during the war years.

The national office had 274 employees, 40 times the number when James E. West opened the new New York headquarters in 1911. They included specialists in education, camping, and publications, as well as 20 field Scout executives who roamed the country helping to organize local councils. Some 40 percent of all troops were under local council jurisdiction, but 9,000 troops still relied on the national office for guidance, literature, badges, and Scouting supplies.

The BSA had earned a place as a vital and growing institution in American life. Now came the task of consolidating the gains and extending Scouting even further. That would require strengthening the local council system, enhancing the training of Scoutmasters, and bringing Scouting to blacks and other minorities.

Two other problems, both related to the fact that boyhood is not a static condition, also nagged at the movement's leaders. The first was the "older boy problem"—what to do about the dropout rate among those who had spent 2 or 3 years in Scouting. The other was what to do about the thousands of boys under age 12 who were clamoring to get into Scouting.

4
Widening Reach

In those days our people were pretty down on their luck from dust storms and the Depression. We had a rule that no one could have a new uniform because we didn't want any boy to feel inadequate or inferior. So we passed around second-hand uniforms and tried to outfit each boy from the hand-me-downs of older brothers. We made our own camping equipment, too—at least some of it. . . . Scouting is a joy—and a challenge. It is fun and fellowship, honor and patriotism.

—Scoutmaster Hubert H. Humphrey of Troop 6, chartered to the Good Fellowship Class of the Methodist Church in Huron, S.Dak., 1933–36; Vice President of the United States, 1965–69

BETWEEN THE END of World War I and the depths of the Great Depression of the 1930's, the Boy Scouts of America reached out to rural and minority youth and settled into the organizational structure that continues today. At the same time, a beginning was made on a separate program for younger boys and the seed that would become Exploring for older youths was germinating in Boy Scouting.

The local council system was reaching maturity during the twenties; by 1930 only 2 percent of the nation's 28,000 troops still depended on the national office for service. Training of Scoutmasters and professional Scouters was being upgraded, too. In 1923 Chief Scout Executive James E. West could proudly report that 350 local councils and 45 colleges offered

Hard times during the Depression are reflected in a newspaper cartoon.

This 1930 Life *cartoon by Charles Dana Gibson carried the caption, "You'll do."*

97

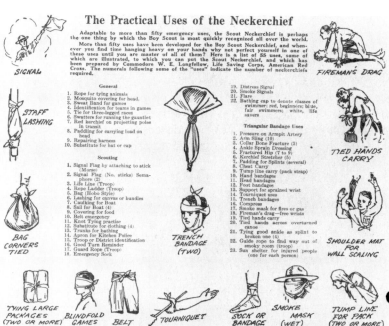

"There isn't a handsomer sight in the world than a patrol or troop of boys in the Official Scout Uniform," proclaimed this official BSA catalog (this page and opposite) in 1925.

SCOUT OUTFIT F—Woolen
Complete, $21.30

Scoutmasters' training courses. The first national conference of professional executives had been held 3 years earlier.

West was less pleased with membership gains in the years after the war. Membership had soared by 45 percent in 1917 and by another 17 percent the following year. In the postwar years, gains dropped into the 5–10 percent range. For this reason, and because West and the other national leaders genuinely wanted to bring Scouting to all boys, they began looking toward rural boys and blacks and other minorities.

Sixty percent of America's villages and small towns still had no Scout troop. West thought the BSA should do better. The result was appointment of a Committee on Rural Scouting, which developed 38 new merit badges on farm-related subjects and secured help from 4-H clubs, Granges, and county agents in organizing troops. The rural effort was enhanced by "railroad Scouting"—a unique method of organizing practiced by railroad men. By 1927 eight railroads had employees whose chief duty was to start troops in small towns along the line. The railroad's interest was in cutting down vandalism of railroad property by providing a healthy outlet for youthful spirits. Although considerable effort was put into promotion of rural Scouting, the BSA's biggest influx of rural boys came in 1924 when the 45,000 members of the Lone Scouts of America were absorbed.

During Scouting's formative years, segregation of blacks—and, to a lesser extent, of other minorities—was law in the South and custom in many other sections of the country. The Boy Scouts of America never drew a color line, but the movement stayed in step with prevailing mores. In the Deep South, Scouting was as segregated as the schools and other public accommodations until the civil rights revolution following the Supreme Court's *Brown* v. *Board of Education* decision in 1954. But there was at least one integrated troop in the Deep South 8 years before *Brown*. In 1946, Scoutmaster Bill B. Lowlar had two black Scouts in Troop 9 in an all-white housing project in Montgomery, Ala. The blacks lived near the project, and Lowlar remembered, "We were kind of looked down on for having those two in the troop. A lot of people were wondering how we could do that, but they were as good workers and as good Scouts as the rest of them." He added, "There was no dissension in the troop whatsoever."

In the North integrated troops were not uncommon in Scouting's early days. A. J. Stilwell, who joined Troop 1 in Dowagiac, Mich., in 1914, said the troop included two black Scouts. And in 1916, Charles S. Hollander, a part-time professional Scouter, organized an integrated troop in a public school for the deaf in Newark, N.J.

But Scouting was slow in coming to black boys, especially in the South —although there was a black troop in Elizabeth City, N.C., in 1911 and others in Nashville and Memphis by 1913. Three years later the Louisville, Ky., Council became the first to promote Scouting among blacks and soon had four troops. In 1926 a survey found 249 black troops around the country, with a total membership of 4,923. Louisville had 30 black troops by that time; Chicago had 26; Washington, 10; and Brooklyn, 8.

The National Council authorized an experimental program to encourage local councils, particularly in the South where the vast majority of the nation's blacks lived, to start troops for them. An Inter-Racial Service was set up, and Stanley A. Harris and other professional organizers were sent into the South. By 1934 only one council in the Deep South (Mississippi) was still holding out. A number of councils had held camporees, Scout circuses, and other events for black Scouts, but only 2 percent of all Scout-age blacks were enrolled in troops.

In the Deep South in those days, blacks were second-class citizens in Scouting as well as in public accommodations. Arthur J. H. Clement, Jr., recalled that when black Scouting was developing in Charleston, S.C., in the late 1930's, a special district was set up for black troops. "Our Palmetto District covered the whole council for Negro troops," he said. "We operated parallel to the council, with our own president, commissioners, and so forth. We had a separate camp for the Negro boys; it wasn't second-class—it was about sixth class. It had a water hole and one or two shacks or sheds on it."

In some parts of the South, black Scouts could not wear the uniform. Some troops wore identifying armbands and the campaign hat. In others, they dressed in white shirts and trousers. By the late 1930's black Scouts in most cities of the South were permitted to buy the uniform and Scouting commenced a slow growth in black communities.

The Scouting movement's willingness to accept boys of all races and creeds—if only in segregated troops—enraged white supremacists like the night-riding Ku Klux Klan. The Klan, which had terrorized former slaves

Outfit H $8.95 Complete

after the Civil War, had a renaissance during the 1920's and became a political power in many states, including several in the North. By that time, the Klan was seeking to intimidate Jews, Roman Catholics, and foreigners as well as blacks.

In 1924 hooded Klansmen fired shots and burned a fiery cross at a camp of black Scouts near Upper Darby, Pa., and ordered the camp evacuated. Three years later a Klan speaker in Freeport, N.Y., urged parents not to let their sons join the Boy Scouts because, he said, they were under control of the Catholic Church.

The Klan virtually ruled Indiana for a time during the 1920's, and as one result Julian H. Salomon was forced out as Scout executive in Terre Haute. He had hired a Catholic seminarian as summer camp aide, and when the Klan heard about it, Salomon was pressured to fire him. Salomon refused and was transferred to another council.

The BSA's Inter-Racial Service effort was directed mainly toward black youth but it also promoted Scouting in Indian schools and reservations and among Mexican youth along the Rio Grande and Japanese boys on the West Coast. Not all Scouting among Indian boys was under the aegis of the Service, however; sometimes it sprang up unaided. Kurttle J. Karlinsey recalled that as a 17-year-old Boy Scout in Lander, Wyo., he became acting Scoutmaster for 16 Shoshone Indian boys. They had left the reservation for the school year to board in town and attend high school.

"I remember these kids used to come to meetings of my troop," he said. "They'd sit off by themselves, and they just melted me down. I held out for a while, and then I organized them into a troop." There was much prejudice against Indians among the town's white adults, Karlinsey said, "because Lander had been right smack dab in the middle of the Indian wars, and there were men living who had fought them." But, he added, the white Scouts did not share the prejudice. Karlinsey's Indian troop turned out to be camporee champions because the boys were wizards at tracking, trailing, pitching tents, cooking without utensils, and nature lore. They were indifferent to rank advancement. "They couldn't understand why a white man had to achieve rank in order to get anything done," Karlinsey explained.

While the Boy Scouts of America was extending its reach to include more rural and minority-group boys, it was also seeking ways to hold onto older Scouts. Thirty percent of all Boy Scouts were 15 or older—a much higher proportion than today—but national leaders were dissatisfied with the dropout rate.

Thus, the "older boy problem." Sea Scouting, for boys over the age of 14, had been operating on a small scale since 1911 when ships were formed in Waltham, Mass., and Philadelphia, but it had the built-in limitation of requiring a vessel and access to a respectable body of water. Despite that limitation, Sea Scouting thrived in some unlikely places; in the mid-1930's, 413 of the 539 local councils had at least one Sea Scout ship.

Typical of the inland sailors was Ship 101 of Altoona in the mountains of central Pennsylvania. The nearest lake was 40 miles away at a Scout camp near Huntingdon, but Ship 101's Sea Scouts went there regularly to sail a fleet of 20 boy-built kayaks and sailboats. The ship's meeting place

This Cub Scout pack was organized in 1929, a year before the BSA began its official Cub Scouting program.

was a large basement room in a church-owned building. Jack Isenberg recalled, "We made that room like the interior of a ship. We had a bridge and a forecastle, and the stern was more or less a big meeting room. We had one fellow who was a very good artist and he painted scenes of ships along the walls. And we got all sorts of things from the Navy and Coast Guard—anchors and binnacles—and put them in that room."

Good Scoutmasters had long been using older Scouts as junior leaders. This was recognized in 1925 when the position of junior assistant Scoutmaster was created. Still the hemorrhage of older Scouts continued, and the National Council began casting about for a separate program for them.

In Utah, the Church of Jesus Christ of Latter-day Saints (Mormon) was worrying about the dropout rate, too. In 1924 the Salt Lake Council began holding annual Older Scout Conferences to exhort its senior Scouts to stay in Scouting. Out of these conferences grew the church's Vanguards for 15- and 16-year-old boys. Beginning in 1928, Vanguards were placed in separate troops for advanced camping, hiking, archery, fishing, and other activities in Indian lore, athletics, electricity, and merit badge projects.

Similar units for older Scouts appeared during the early thirties elsewhere in the West, particularly in Portland, Ore., and Seattle, Wash. In Portland they were known as Scout Foresters, Engineers, and Rangers and wore uniforms combining parts of BSA and Canadian Scout regalia. By 1936 they and the Mormons' Vanguards were being referred to as Explorer Scouts. Some Explorer Scouts formed patrols within Boy Scout troops; others were in separate units.

An import from England called Rover Scouting was also seen as a possible answer to the older boy problem, although Rovers were older than Explorer Scouts. Rovering was for young men from 18 to 25 years old.

These early Cubs, gathered in Stamford, Conn., in 1921 or 1922, had to rely on British Cub books and programs.

The first black troop in Virginia, in 1928, led by Maceo Johnson, left.

Rover crews were essentially service groups for troops and councils. They began appearing in 1928 in the West, and the following year crews were organized in Rochester, N.Y., and the Boston area.

Among the early organizers of Rovering was Rod Speirs, a native of England who came to the United States in 1930 and became a professional Scouter here. He said the early crews followed the plan outlined in *Rovering to Success*, by Scouting's founder, Baden-Powell. Induction into a crew was modeled on a knighthood ceremony. The candidate undertook a night-long vigil similar to that of today's Order of the Arrow, followed the next day by a formal investiture.

"In the Leif Ericsson crew in the Norumbega Council near Boston, we ran campfires at the council camp and acted as aides for big council events," Speirs said. Rovers also helped their communities by, for example, donating blood at hospitals. In New England, Rover crews held conferences called moots to discuss service projects, how to train Rover candidates, and other questions.

Some Scout leaders improvised a program for older Scouts. In Portland, Ore., the 15 older boys in Scoutmaster Everett M. Royce's Troop 20 dubbed themselves the Musketeers, created an induction ritual using foils and sabers, and adopted parts of Rovering. They held 3-hour meetings, half devoted to the troop, which was chartered to the First Methodist Church, and half to Rovering. "We also were judges at rallies and Scout field meets," Royce said. "Otherwise, we did mostly mountain climbing."

Rovering became an official program of the Boy Scouts of America in 1933 but it never took fire. At its peak about 1940, there were about 2,000 Rover Scouts. Rovering's numbers were decimated when its members went off to fight in World War II but it lingered on for a time after the war.

Senior Scouting, a plan for advanced Scouting within the troop, also developed during the 1920's. During and after World War II, the streams of Explorer Scouting, Senior Scouting, and Rovering would merge into the beginnings of modern Exploring.

The national leaders of the BSA also faced pressure from the other end of the age spectrum—boys under 12 years old. Younger boys had been clamoring to join from the time of Scouting's birth in this country, and, in fact, some were in Scouting at the beginning.

The "younger boy problem" started with an innocuous sentence in Ernest Thompson Seton's 1910 Manual for Scouts. That book stated that Scouts were 12 to 18 years old, but it also said, "In special cases boys nine years old may become tenderfeet." What the special cases were was not explained, but many early troops enrolled young boys. In 1911, at the urging of Chief Scout Executive James E. West, the national Executive Board ruled that Scouts must be at least 12 years old but it did not expel the younger scouts. (Expulsion would have been impossible to enforce anyway, because until 1913 Boy Scouts were not registered.)

For nearly 2 decades, the BSA had no program for the younger boys. There was, however, much talk about the problem and one tentative move toward a program. After setting the 12-year age minimum for Boy Scouting, the Executive Board asked Chief Scout Seton to create a program for younger boys. He promptly produced a workable plan called Cubs of America. His plan called for a bear cub as the organization's symbol. Boys would be organized into Cub rings with a Cub mother as leader. Seton suggested the motto, "We do our best"—just a hair's breadth from the motto later adopted for Cub Scouts (We'll do our best).

Seton's influence was already waning in the National Council, though, and Cubs of America never was tried. Meanwhile, in England, Baden-Powell was working out a special program for younger boys. He drew symbols from *The Jungle Book* by Rudyard Kipling, a famous author and poet who was also a commissioner in British Scouting. In 1916 Wolf Cubbing became a part of the British Scouting program with publication of *The Wolf Cub's Handbook*, which outlined a program of simple Scouting activities suitable for boys under 12 years of age. A Wolf Cub pack was made up of several groups called sixes and was led by either a male or female Cubmaster. Wolf Cubs could earn the ranks of Tenderpad, One-Star Cub, and Two-Star Cub.

Like Baden-Powell's *Scouting for Boys*, *The Wolf Cub's Handbook* quickly made the transatlantic crossing and was the guide for many packs in the United States and Canada. A pack was formed as early as 1918 in Butte, Mont., and during the 1920's many packs appeared using the British Wolf Cub plan or a Canadian adaptation.

From 1921 to 1925, Douglas Beals was a Wolf Cub in the Congregational Church in Bristol, Conn. "The church's youth director was Pauline Chaulker, an English lady, and she organized some 20 boys into this group," Beals remembered. "We had regular weekly meetings. There was a certain amount of training in the social arts—being a nice guy, learning to be polite and so forth—as part of being a Wolf Cub. We were into such things as craftwork, which didn't interest me too much. But there was a lot

Scouts stage a cross-country motor tour in 1935 to promote highway safety.

I REMEMBER . . .

The Scene: *Williamsburg section of Brooklyn, N.Y., 1923*

Two or three weeks after I joined Troop 26 at the YMCA, the troop was going on an overnight hike. I'd never been on a hike. The only time I saw a tree was in Prospect Park.

The troop left on overnight hikes after the meeting on Friday nights. So I went home after the troop meeting and picked up the things I needed for the hike, and I was about to go out the door when my mother caught me. She asked where I was going, and I told her I was going out on a camping trip. She really raised the roof! She thought I was running away from home. I said, "Ma, come with me and I'll show you who I'm going with." So I took her to the Y and introduced her to the acting Scoutmaster. He convinced her that it was all right, that he was going to take us out to the country, and that they'd have meals for us—all I needed was carfare.   —*Morris Slotkin*

of outdoor stuff, which *did* interest me. We went on a lot of hikes, she being the typical English lady who tramps the moors and glens, and she'd be with us with her walking staff, whipping the boys along." The Bristol Cubs wore blue uniforms evidently designed by Miss Chaulker.

In Memphis, Tenn., a Wolf Cub pack was started by a young man in the neighborhood where Henry Gardner Colby was living. Colby recalled outdoor meetings with games and an occasional campout near Memphis. The pack used *The Wolf Cub's Handbook* but had no uniforms.

Seattle was a hotbed of early Wolf Cubbing, probably due to its proximity to Canada, where the program was flourishing. The Seattle Council in effect adopted Wolf Cubbing, despite the displeasure of Chief Scout Executive West, and even built a camp for Cubs. The pioneer in Seattle Cubbing was Sol G. Levy, a transplanted Englishman who got a Rotary Club to sponsor the first pack there in 1923.

Another council that encouraged Cubbing was in Stamford, Conn. It also had summer camp for Wolf Cubs. In Derby, Conn., Edmund D. Strang was a 17-year-old Boy Scout patrol leader in 1927 when he formed an informal pack of the youngsters who hung around his troop. A year later he heard about Wolf Cubbing, sent for the literature, and made it into a Wolf Cub pack. Strang remembered, "The Wolf Cub program was like junior Scouting. There was a little knot-tying and little bit of other things the kids would eventually use in Scouting."

Other Wolf Cub packs during the 1920's, all using the British or Canadian plan, were in Detroit, Chicago, Houston, Baltimore, Norfolk, Va., Kansas City, Mo., Rochester and Ithaca, N.Y., and Lamoni, Iowa. Chief Scout Executive West made sure, though, that Wolf Cubbing would not get out of hand by taking the American copyright on *The Wolf Cub's Handbook* in 1918. For 12 years the national Supply Service sold the book, even though Wolf Cubbing was not an approved program.

West had resisted demands for a program for younger boys for two reasons. First, he feared that a second program would burden the movement with new problems while it was still in its adolescence. Second, he believed the "the great need for boy work in America is with the boys 13, 14, 15 and 16 years of age. That is the time," he said, "when the home, the church and other institutions have difficulty in holding them and making effective those values and influences which make for character building and citizenship training." (Later studies indicated that the years from 8 to 12 are the vital ones for molding character and values.) West was joined in opposition to Cubbing by National Scout Commissioner Daniel Carter Beard. He was apparently influenced by anti-British sentiment around the time of World War I, and he also thought the term "Cub" derogatory to boys.

Wolf Cubbing was not the only program available for boys under 12 years old. Ernest Thompson Seton's Woodcraft League was still in the field. In the Piedmont, Calif., Scout Council, there were youngsters called Boy Pioneers—no relation to Dan Beard's old Pioneers. In Portsmouth, Va., and New York City, there were small groups of younger boys called American Eagles, and in Ventura, Calif., there were American Eaglets. Jersey City, N.J., was home to 300 younger boys in the American Tribesmen.

The Tribesmen were perhaps typical of these small groups. Tribes were headed by an adult Chief and sponsored by religious institutions. Each tribe had Little Chiefs, often Boy Scouts. By passing simple tests, the young Tribesman could earn badges for Buck, Hunter, and Brave and aspire to the office of Sachem, or leader of subgroups in the tribe.

Patterned closely on Boy Scouting was a larger organization called the Boy Rangers of America, which was founded in 1913 by Emerson Brooks,

Eagle Scout Paul Siple sailed to Antarctica with Commander Byrd in 1928. At left, he salutes with Chief Scout Executive West.

a retired businessman, in Montclair, N.J. Boy Rangers "played Indian" and practiced pioneering skills. Their "Great Laws" copied the Scout Law. The Boy Rangers aimed to graduate members into Boy Scouting, Seton's Woodcraft program, or Boys' Clubs. At its peak in the mid-1920's, the Boy Rangers had 8,000 members and 700 lodges in 47 states.

Hundreds of Boy Scout troops sheltered "junior Scouts," "trailers," and "mascots." Among them was Troop 128 of the Advocate Lutheran Church in Philadelphia, which had a junior patrol of eight younger boys during the 1920's. "We did almost everything the regular Scouts did, including going to camp for two weeks," said Sylvan P. Stern. "We weren't registered, and we had no uniforms or badges—just khaki clothes—and when the Scouts had instruction, we went off and played games."

After some years of urging by parents and professional Scouters, the national Executive Board in 1924 approved the idea of a program for boys 9 to 11 years old. Dr. H. W. Hurt, a veteran Scouter and educator, was named to develop it. For the next 5 years, Hurt studied existing organizations and worked out a plan for the new program. He received considerable help from Seton, whose antipathy to West did not prevent him from aiding the Boy Scouts of America.

Cub Scouting historian Ann W. Nally believes the major elements that went into the new program came from Baden-Powell's Wolf Cubbing, Seton's Woodcraft program, and the Boy Rangers of America. Cubbing (the term "Cub Scouting" came into use years later) was less oriented toward Boy Scout skills than the English program and drew its symbols from American Indian lore rather than *The Jungle Book*.

The organizational structure was similar to today's Cub Scouting, with one major exception: dens were to be led by a Boy Scout called the den chief rather than by an adult. The plan called for a mother's neighborhood committee to "encourage" Cubs, but mothers were to remain in the background. Dens were to meet weekly for games, crafts, and ceremonies. Two or more dens made up a pack under the leadership of a male Cubmaster and met weekly or semimonthly for games, den competitions, stunts, advancement awards, and other activities. A boy could join at 9 years old as a Bobcat, advance to Wolf in his first year, and earn the Bear badge at age 10 and the Lion at 11 before graduating into a Boy Scout troop.

In August 1929 the new Cubbing program was introduced as a demonstration project in several cities in the Northeast. At the same time, it was being evaluated by 13,500 Scouters, psychologists, educators, and recreation and welfare leaders. Most of the evaluators were Scoutmasters, many of whom doubled as Cubmasters.

Cubbing became official April 1, 1930, with issuance of the first pack charters. By the end of the year, 5,102 Cubs were enrolled.

Boys who were growing up in the twenties and thirties found just as much fun and excitement in Scouting as had the first Scouts in 1910. A few of them reminisce.

Dr. E. S. Ewing, who joined Troop 9, chartered to Irvington Methodist Episcopal Church in Indianapolis, Ind., in 1920:

"We went to our council's camp as individuals, not as a troop. There

Top, a letter by Baden-Powell published in Christian Science Monitor *during a world jamboree in England; above, B-P pins merit badges on Chicago Scouts in 1926.*

were eight boys to a tent, and a 15-to-18 year-old boy would be the head of the tent. We would be awakened in the morning by a bugle and the firing of a small cannon, and we would come out with a towel around us and do our calisthenics. Then we would run down to the creek and jump in for a skinny-dip. We'd go back to the tent and get dressed for raising the colors and then march behind a drummer to the dining hall. Then we would have our craft and skill classes, with a morning swim and an afternoon swim in the creek. After supper there would be a parade of the entire camp before the officers, and then free time and a campfire."

Joseph D. Pickle, member of Troop 1, chartered to the Railroad YMCA, Big Spring, Tex., in 1922:

"Our Scouting was pretty primitive; about all we had to go on was the handbook. It was written about fields and streams and woods, but there aren't many trees in West Texas. I remember that some people sent here for training courses talked about cutting down trees, and we said 'You know what we use for wood out here? We use cow chips.' We just played it by ear, and we had to do a lot of adapting. That's Scouting at work, you know. The principles of Scouting we applied here just like you would anywhere else, but some of the mechanics of it we had to adapt to our region and our customs. Hiking and camping were the heart and soul of it. In the earliest days the troop camped about 35 miles south of here on the Big Concho. They put their heavy gear and chuck on a horse-drawn wagon, and the boys walked. They hiked from water well to water well, and about halfway they'd camp overnight."

Don J. Breining, Troop 61, of the Willard Elementary School PTA, Minneapolis, in 1927:

"Frequently we would camp about 25 miles out on the Willow River in a big cow pasture. Having an ex-Marine as Scoutmaster, we posted guards all night long. It scared the dickens out of us when the cows came over in the middle of the night and started nosing around. I can remember chasing cows away from our tents."

Robert C. Koerner, Troop 129, chartered to St. George's Roman Catholic Church, St. Louis, in 1929:

"Scouting was like a million bucks. You could go out just a few miles from the city then and chop a tree, make a fire, and camp almost anywhere. In the summer, by the time I got to be a junior leader, a buddy and I would go out for 2 weeks at a time, come home for a week, and then go out again. Sometimes we'd take two or three patrols with us. We'd conduct all our activities; there wasn't any adult with us. Our parents and Scoutmaster didn't worry about us. We were trained."

During the twenties and thirties, the well-dressed Boy Scout looked less like a soldier than his older brother had. In 1919 the official uniform was modified, notably by the addition of a neckerchief and substitution of knee-length stockings for the old canvas leggings. The breeches remained standard. Bermuda-length shorts were available, too, but rarely seen. The national office encouraged their use, particularly for camping. But when shorts were prescribed attire at an executives' conference in 1920 they "caused a merriment as well as interest," West reported, and it was years before shorts were fully accepted.

A Scout admires his classic jamboree lunch: a hot dog roasted on a stick.

From the recollections of old Scouts, it is likely that only troops in affluent communities were fully uniformed. After the stock market crash in October 1929, even fewer Boy Scouts boasted full regalia. The Great Depression which followed the crash, reaching its devastating peak in 1931 when a quarter of American workers had no jobs, brought the nation's economic life to a virtual standstill. The Boy Scouts of America was not exempt from hardship.

During the Depression years, weekly dues in most troops were a nickel. For overnight camping, meals were often potluck, using whatever ingredients the Scouts could bring. Scoutmaster Howard Carl remembered that in Muscatine, Iowa's, Troop 134, "One boy would go to a meat shop and get soup bones for nothing, and we all brought stuff from our vegetable gardens. One kid might bring 15 cents worth of boiling beef, and we'd cook it all in the same pot and enjoy the same thing."

In Troop 67 of the Rosemont Christian Church in Dallas, 50 cents was charged for three meals on an overnight camp. "But," said John Kilgore, "a lot of the guys didn't have 50 cents so they'd bring some potatoes out of the family larder."

"We really had to tighten our belts," said John L'Abbe of the Congregational Church's Troop 21 in Tomahawk, Wis. "I can recall that for the Second Class cooking test you had to cook a quarter-pound of steak. A lot of the boys said, 'I'd better make it this time because I'm not going to get another piece if this one is spoiled.' "

Future Vice President Hubert Humphrey leads a troop in South Dakota in 1934. Uniforms were scarce due to the Depression.

Evelyn Loman, the 6-year-old daughter of a San Diego Scoutmaster, hands over a $25 war bond she bought selling bottles and rags with Scouts.

A week in a local council's summer camp cost $5 to $10, depending on the region. In Hamden, Conn., the Scouts of Troop 1 couldn't afford even those modest fees so they camped for a week in woods owned by Scoutmaster Norman A. Greist. "The senior patrol leader was in charge," Greist recalled. "I was out there for supper and the evening program but not for the rest of the day. They got along fine."

Staff salaries in the national office were cut 15 percent. Many local councils were forced to merge, lay off employees, or slash wages; some Scout executives worked for a time without pay. Henry N. Brown III was one of the lucky ones. He had just become Scout executive in Orlando, Fla., in March 1933 when the council's funds were frozen in a bank moratorium, but he continued to draw a salary. "We pulled through largely, I guess, because I didn't know any better and just bluffed it out," he said. He had to lay off the council's only other employee, a secretary, and for a time he did all the office work as well as overseeing Scouting in five counties. "I struggled along," he said.

The election of Franklin D. Roosevelt in 1932 on a New Deal platform brought hope to the nation's unemployed. It also brought the BSA's first large-scale Good Turn since World War I. In a radio address in February 1934, Roosevelt called on the Boy Scouts of America to gather household furnishings, clothing, and other items to help the needy. Thousands of troops responded, collecting more than 1.8 million of the requested articles.

"It was one of the first Good Turns that I got involved in," said Saul Gilbert, who was a member of Troop 90, chartered to a Group of Citizens

Scouts present a 90th-birthday cake to "Uncle Dan" Beard in 1940. The aged Scouting pioneer lived only one more year after this picture was taken.

in Brooklyn, N.Y. "It's a rather vivid memory even today" he said, "because I was going into tenement homes where they were more in need of receiving than giving. But they were generous to the extent that they could be." Similar scenes were enacted all around the country as Boy Scouts knocked on doors and came away with a pair of shoes, an old blanket, a child's shirt, or a used chair.

Some troops continued Good Turns for the poor throughout the Depression years. In Staten Island, N.Y., for example, Scoutmaster Frederick Franzwick's troop regularly gathered milk bottles to get the deposit on them, and earned about $20 a week, which the troop committee distributed to the needy. Other troops made up Thanksgiving and Christmas baskets each year to give to the unemployed.

Men who were Boy Scouts during the Depression remember less of the hardships than the fun of Scouting. They were, after all, boys, and almost everyone was in the same economic straits. It was quite normal to have no money, to have only a neckerchief and perhaps a Scout shirt and to contribute only a few carrots or potatoes to the troop's chuck on a campout.

And still boys flocked to join Scouting. At the end of 1934, membership in the Boy Scouts of America was nearing one million.

Norman Rockwell
Lends a Helping Hand

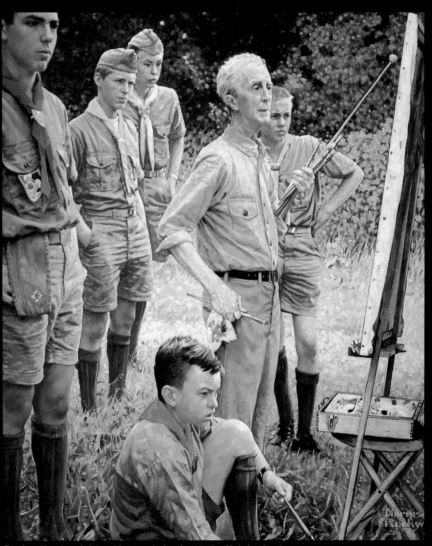

Rockwell painted this self-portrait for the 1969 official calendar.

Helping Define Scouting

One day in the fall of 1912, a talented 18-year-old art student named Norman Rockwell walked into the offices of *Boy's Life* looking for work. When he left, he had his first commission to do a magazine illustration—and had begun a relationship with the Boy Scouts of America that would last for more than 60 years. Rockwell became the visual spokesman for Scouting, bringing its spirit and ideals to life through hundreds of now-classic paintings.

On My Honor *(left), 1953, illustrates the Scout Oath.*
In A Scout Is Helpful *(below), 1941, a flood victim is aided.*

A Scout Is Friendly, *1943.*

A Patriotic Vision

When the gangly Rockwell tried to join the Navy to fight in World War I, in 1917, he was at first rejected for being 17 pounds underweight. He later made it in—with the help of a Navy doctor who waived a rule for him—but then found himself doing "morale" work at a base in Charleston, S. C., preparing art for the camp newspaper and painting and sketching officers and sailors. Throughout his life, he remained deeply patriotic, and he frequently used heroic symbols, especially the American flag, to communicate patriotic values to Boy Scouts. The painting at right honored the 200th birthday of George Washington; the one below honored that of the nation.

Above, The Spirit of '76, *1976.*
Right, A Scout Is Loyal, *1932.*

A Scout helps an old man across the street in The Daily Good Turn, *1918.*

Good Deeds Through the Years

Every year but two from 1925 through 1976, Norman Rockwell did a painting for the annual Boy Scout calendar published by Brown & Bigelow. Each painting, including the two on this page, presented an image of idealized Scouts in worthy action—and always with meticulously accurate uniforms and equipment. By 1929, the Boy Scout calendar was the most popular in America, and it remained so for many years.

All Together, *1947: a helping hand.*

In Friend in Need, *1949, the Scout gives a small friend first aid.*

Scouting Makes Real Men Out of Boys, *1918, salutes Scouts who acted as lookouts and signaled messages for the Navy along the Atlantic Coast during World War I.*

Scouting in Action

Asked if he might ever run out of subjects for his paintings, Rockwell once said, "The Boy Scouts are simply going to have to devise some new deeds or Brown & Bigelow will be in a stew." Yet the artist always found fresh ways to evoke the virtues of Scouting—in the work below, he simply catches the excitement of a troop heading out on a camping trip. In 1939—when he had been painting Scouts for more than 25 years —Rockwell was honored with the highest award given by the Boy Scouts of America, the Silver Buffalo, presented before an audience of 3,000 people at the Waldorf-Astoria in New York.

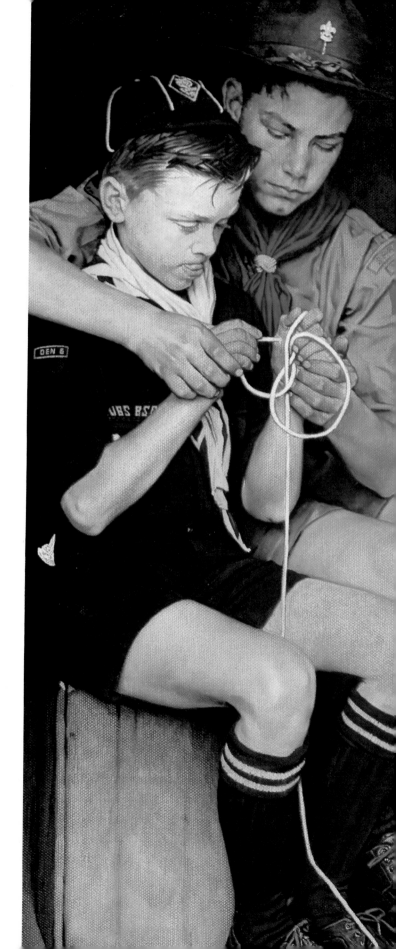

Scouting Is Outing (*above*), *1968, and* A Guiding Hand (*right*), *1946, were both done for the annual calendar.*

Scouting Around the World

In the sixties, Rockwell's focus broadened to include many more minority and foreign Scouts. His calendar paintings for the world jamboree years of 1963 and 1967, shown here, both depicted Scouts of various nations joyously united. *A Good Sign All Over the World* (opposite) shows two Scottish Scouts and an American being cheered on by an Indonesian and an Indian; approaching on the right are Jamaican, Canadian, and Lebanese Scouts.

Breakthrough for Freedom, *1967.*

A Good Sign All Over the World, *1963.*

Leaders of the Troops

In these two paintings of Scoutmasters at work, Rockwell demonstrates his rare ability to take an unsurprising scene and imbue it with magic. "The commonplaces of America are to me the richest subjects in art," he once said. "Boys batting flies on vacant lots; girls playing jacks on front steps; old men plodding home at twilight—all these arouse feelings in me."

Straight Talk by Scoutmaster (*left*), *1918, is an early effort in color.*
The Scoutmaster (*below*), *1956, is among Rockwell's most beloved Scout paintings.*

Left: Homecoming, *1961.*
Below: Can't Wait, *1972.*
Opposite: Growth of a Leader,
*1966. Each tells a tale of growing
up happily, portraying the
attainment of maturity through
attainments in Scouting.*

Upward and Onward

Rockwell's illustrations almost defined America in the middle
part of the 20th century; they certainly helped define Scouting.
His career spanned nearly the whole history of the Boy
Scouts to date, encompassing an age during which both
America and the Boy Scouts grew immensely—a period, as
Rockwell wrote, "when America believed in itself. I was happy
to be painting it." The artist died in 1978 at the age of 84.

5
Growing and Serving

The Boy Scouts are so much a part of the American picture that it is hard to believe they have been around for only thirty-five years. They are so tangled up in the vocabulary, humor, ideals and daily life of the nation that one would think they had been around as long as the Grange or the W.C.T.U. . . . Probably the secret is that the Scouts, instead of playing soldier or cops-and-robbers, actually participate in the life of their communities. During the war they have sold Bonds, collected scrap materials, assisted ration boards and other civilian boards. . . . Who can tell how much the Boy Scout movement has done to relieve the blackout of the Seven Ages of Man—those years when a boy is too old to have nothing useful to do and too young to be allowed to do it.—Saturday Evening Post, 1945

"Strong for the sake of America!" read a line at the bottom of this forceful poster.

On December 7, 1941, the United States was plunged into World War II when the Japanese mounted a devastating bombing assault on the U.S. naval base at Pearl Harbor, Hawaii. As it had in World War I, the Boy Scouts of America, along with nearly all Americans, rallied to the war effort.

Boy Scouts were in the thick of things from the start. Although Hawaii was not a state, three local councils of the Boy Scouts of America were operating in the Hawaiian Islands. The Honolulu Council, which included Pearl Harbor, mobilized hundreds of Scouts after the attack on the Pacific Fleet. Even during the bombing, 40 Scouts and leaders were fighting fires

This World War II poster urged churches, schools, and clubs to organize new Scout troops.

and guarding roads, and 14 Sea Scouts were aiding Honolulu's police in emergency duties.

In the days after Pearl Harbor, Hawaiian Scouts gave valiant service, working as aides and messengers to civil authorities, helping police with traffic control, manning first-aid stations, enforcing blackouts at night, aiding in the evacuation of civilians injured in the attack, and assisting at communications centers.

After Pearl Harbor, no U.S. Boy Scouts participated officially in the war at first hand, but their home-front service enhanced the reputation of the BSA as a national resource for service. By the time the war ended with atomic bomb holocausts over Hiroshima and Nagasaki in August 1945, the Boy Scouts of America had responded to 69 requests for help from the government.

In the late Depression years leading up to America's entry into World War II, the BSA was reaching maturity. The administrative structure that enabled the movement to respond quickly to national service needs was fully developed. Hundreds of thousands of Boy Scouts were learning the outdoor and survival skills that would later prove valuable for young men on ship and shore during the war.

The Boy Scouts of America observed its 25th anniversary in 1935, still growing in size and influence. Planned as the centerpiece of the Silver Jubilee was the first national jamboree, which would bring more than 20,000 Scouts and leaders to Washington, D.C., from every state and several foreign countries for a giant encampment.

A Scout at a camporee blows a signal with the horn of a kudu, continuing a tradition started by Baden-Powell at the first gathering at Brownsea.

But it was not to be. An epidemic of polio was reported in the Washington area that summer, and in those days before the development of polio vaccines, the disease—then called infantile paralysis—was one of the most fearsome scourges of childhood. Two weeks before the camp was scheduled to open, the jamboree was canceled in a radio message by President Franklin D. Roosevelt.

"It was a great disappointment," recalled J. Gordon Gurley, a member of the jamboree contingent from Los Angeles. "We'd made all our plans and we had our jamboree neckerchiefs and patches, and there was a lot of confusion." Out of that confusion a plan developed to give the 100 Los Angeles jamboree Scouts a 2-week train tour of the West Coast and Canada. "We lived aboard the train, and it was very exciting for those of us who had never been out of southern California," Gurley said. Elsewhere in the country, derailed jamboree groups were offered similar consolation trips.

The jamboree was rescheduled for 1937 and went off without a hitch. It attracted 27,232 Scouts and Scouters to Washington in the largest gathering of Scouts up to that time.

Boy Scouts who lived in cities during that era were used to big crowds. Often a local council would take over its city's largest arena to stage a Scout show called a circus, roundup, or merit badge show. New York City Scouts twice filled the old Madison Square Garden for shows featuring demonstrations of pioneering and other Scoutcraft skills and such spectaculars as a "living flag" made up of hundreds of boys, each bearing a piece of red, white, or blue cloth, who formed a huge U.S. flag on the floor of the arena.

In Kansas City and St. Louis, Scout shows were annual or semiannual affairs. Robert C. Koerner recalled that in St. Louis the show-stopper was the assembly of a full-scale log cabin in 7 minutes by his Troop 129. "We worked for months getting ready—cutting the logs, trimming, notching, and numbering them and practicing erecting the cabin," he said. "Other troops built towers and other pioneering projects. For the finale of the show, the lights went dim, and when they came up again you had almost a frontier town on the floor of the arena," Koerner said.

In Minneapolis the big shows were called Wallakazoos. "They were citywide competitions in first aid and things of that type and were held in an auditorium," said Don J. Breining, a member of Troop 66. "They would attract three to four thousand people—and not just parents of the Scouts."

Also popular were rallies—smaller-scale public competitions that were forerunners of today's district camporees. "Rallies were big in those days," said Saul Gilbert, who was a Scout in Brooklyn's Troop 90 during the thirties. "They were strictly competitive—Morse, semaphore, knot-tying, first aid, compass, and things of that nature. And there were games—cock fights, crab races, wheelbarrow races. I remember that in knot-tying you usually had to tie 9 knots in 18 seconds to win."

In some Wisconsin cities rallies developed into intercouncil events. "They were really big deals," said Laurence Raymer, a member of Troop 1 in Beloit. "We'd have intercouncil competitions with Madison, Freeport, Elgin, Rockford—even Milwaukee and Eau Claire, Wis. The rallies were held in

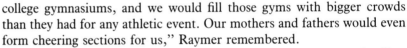

I REMEMBER...

The Scene: *Los Angeles during nationwide aluminum scrap collection, 1941*

Like the other troops in Los Angeles, we had canvassed our neighborhood and come up with aluminum pots and pans and brought them to our Scout hut. The material was picked up and we were assigned to guard this strategic material. So we reported to the old circus headquarters on Washington Boulevard.

This was a very large area and here was an absolute mountain of pots and pans. We were to guard it so that no foreign power could come by in the middle of the night and whisk it away.

We had brought a couple of World War I pup tents, but we stayed up all night because none of us really wanted to sleep. We were just boys, and none of us realized that every one of us would eventually wind up fighting in the war.

—*Raul Chavez*

college gymnasiums, and we would fill those gyms with bigger crowds than they had for any athletic event. Our mothers and fathers would even form cheering sections for us," Raymer remembered.

Scouting's public entertainment was not confined to shows and rallies. Brooklyn's Troop 20 had a drum and bugle corps and a traveling pyramid team. The pyramid-builders were adept at creating living statues and other forms by standing on each other's shoulders. "Our pyramid team performed in all the largest theaters and armories in Brooklyn," recalled Troop 20 Scoutmaster Al R. Dayes.

His troop's drum and bugle corps had counterparts all over the country. In Montgomery, Ala., for example, Henry A. Murray began a 50-year career as a Scouter when he was asked to start a drum and bugle corps for Troop 8. From the 60-member troop, he trained a 30-piece corps to march in parades and play at Scout shows. And in San Francisco, Frank T. Sharpe, a committee member for Pack 100, led a 20-piece drum corps of Cub Scouts that spent its summer weekends marching in parades.

Scout musical groups were not new in the thirties, however. Scores of early Boy Scout troops had small bands. In 1912, Troop 1 in the village of Bethel, Ohio, had a 24-piece marching band led by Big Jim Fitzpatrick, the local postmaster. "He was a great teacher," remembered W. E. Bennington. "We had a band practice as well as a troop meeting each week, and he would give us lessons to learn at home," he said. Fitzpatrick was drum major as well as director, and, said Bennington, "I can still see him strutting and twirling that baton. Should any boy not know his music, he marched but his horn was stuffed up with rags."

Sometimes enthusiasm for music got out of hand. In Oil City, Pa., when Charles M. Heistand arrived to become Scout executive in 1920, he found that half the council's operating budget went for instruments, uniforms, and traveling expenses for a Boy Scout band. The band traveled so often that a railroad car was parked at the station for its use. Heistand, who later became assistant Chief Scout Executive, solved his musical problem by calling in the instruments and band uniforms "for an inventory." "And," he recalled, "I didn't let them go out again."

Membership in the Boy Scouts of America was rising steadily in the Silver Jubilee year. Enrollment of Boy Scouts increased by only 2 percent, but Cubbing was on the march. There were 57,000 Cubs and 950 pack leaders, and scores of packs were being formed every day.

Although Cub Scouting was clearly the wave of the BSA's future growth, some national executives continued to think of the young program as a stepchild. Membership figures for Cubbing were lumped in with the records for Boy Scouts, as if Cubbing were merely the tail on the dog and shouldn't wag at all. At a conference of Scout executives in 1936, William C. Wessel, Cubbing's first national director, noticed that on charts showing national statistics, all totals that included Cubs were marked with an asterisk. He and another professional stealthily turned each asterisk into a daisy. After that, Cubbing got its own standing in all national statistics.

Chief Scout Executive West, who had dragged his heels in the face of early demands for a program for younger boys, cheerfully ate crow as Cubbing grew and prospered. One of his concerns had been that Cubbing would infringe on Boy Scouting; this was by no means unlikely because many of the early Cubmasters were also Scoutmasters. There were frequent admonitions from the national office like this one in 1932: "We must keep Cubbing sharply different from Scouting in order not to unconsciously imitate or parallel Scouting. Keep Cubbing different! Keep it home-centered!"

Whether because of such exclamation-pointed advice or because Cubbing's advancement program was distinctly different from Boy Scouting's, the

The emblem opposite was designed for a 1935 jamboree that had to be postponed due to a polio outbreak. Scouts finally pitched their tents near the Washington Monument for that jamboree (this page) in 1937.

new program soon established its own identity. Herbert Birch, who founded a pack in Trenton, N.J., in 1932 while he was also Scoutmaster of a troop in Tenafly, 70 miles away, recalled that at first his pack offered junior Scouting but gradually shifted into the Cubbing program. Ben Havilland, who joined Pack 1 in Seattle in 1934—a year after it had converted from the Canadian Cubbing program—remembered that Cubbing was very similar to Cub Scouting today. But, he added, "in those days we also had a lot of interpack athletics—touch football and roller skating and softball—and we went to camp for a full week when I was 10 or 11 years old."

Ben Havilland's experience of camping as a Cub Scout was not unique. James Fritze, who became a Cub in 1934 on Staten Island, N.Y., recalled that his pack had overnight campouts two or three times a year at a local Scout camp. At about the same time, Cubs in Decatur, Ill., spent a week in Scout camp enjoying games, swimming, and boating. Dan O. Henry, who later became Scout executive of the Greater New York Councils, remembered, "It came about because the Scout executive needed to balance the summer camp budget. The Cubs survived all right. I don't remember that we had any more homesickness with those Cubs than with Boy Scouts."

Each Cub pack was divided into subgroups of six to ten boys called dens. In early Cubbing literature, it was recommended that dens be led by Boy Scouts called den chiefs. That was the case in the Milwaukee suburb of Shorewood where Henry G. Kreiner, who was a den chief, recalled, "We more or less ran the program for den meetings. But of course there was supervision by mothers because we generally met in the homes of the Cubs, and we were responsible to the mothers."

More often than not, the mothers were the de facto den leaders, especially when the den chief was not mature enough to handle a horde of young boys by himself. In 1932, with publication of the first *Cubmaster's Handbook* and *Den Chief's Denbook*, the "den mother" was recognized as a member of the den leadership team, although she merely "shared" leadership with the den chief as his adviser and guide. On paper she was the liaison between the den and a neighborhood parents' committee.

Experience showed, though, that dens operated best with den mothers in charge. Bowing to the realities, the national Executive Board approved optional registration of den mothers in 1936, but they were not required to register until 12 years later. In the first *Den Mother's Denbook*, published in 1936, the den mother was advised to "keep somewhat in the background—making the den chief the important figure in the den meeting."

Even with her secondary status, the den mother was told that she should be a paragon of virtues with "(1) an even temper; (2) a kindly and not too distant friendliness; (3) a quick, buoyant smile; (4) a sense of humor, especially if the joke be on her—which might be expected at times; (5) much patience and hope; (6) a recognition that normal boys are increasingly different from normal girls and probably less quiet and more active; (7) tact in dealing with people—old and young; and (8) ability to put one's self in the other's shoes."

All Cubmasters and pack committee members were supposed to be men, but many early packs had women leaders. In 1931 the National Executive

Scouts in Gastonia, N. C., display one of 24 stretchers they built for emergency hospitals.

Board considered registering women as Cubmasters but decided against it; packs that were in fact led by women had to show a male Cubmaster on their registration forms.

The first Cubbing handbook, titled *The Boy's Cubbook*, was published while the first packs were being chartered in 1930. The book was quickly revised when it was noted that the Cubbing sign (then the Indian "How" with upraised palm) was disconcertingly like the Nazi salute of Adolf Hitler, who was then beginning his rise to power in Germany. The sign was hastily changed to the gesture that became popular during World War II as Winston Churchill's V-for-victory. In Cub Scouting, the upraised index and middle fingers symbolized the ears of an alert wolf.

The original Cub uniform was blue trimmed in gold and cost $6.05, including belt. The shirt was either a pocketless jersey or a two-pocket dress shirt topped by a gold neckerchief bordered in blue. Cubs wore knickers or shorts with knee-length blue stockings rimmed at the top with two gold stripes. The cap was a beanie with a tiny visor; centered in front was the universal Cub emblem—a Bobcat badge.

Cubs wore only their current badge of rank and any arrow points they had earned for extra work on that badge; the practice of wearing all earned badges began in 1941. (But the first Cubs could wear all their Cub badges on their merit badge sashes when they became Boy Scouts.) The early graduates into troops were the first "Cub Scouts"; in those days a Cub Scout was a Boy Scout who had been a Cub.

Cubbing grew rapidly during its first decade. By the time of Pearl Harbor in 1941, there were 270,000 Cubs and leaders—less than a quarter of the number in Boy Scouting, but Cubbing was closing fast.

Nearly all of these New Jersey Scouts, photographed in 1940, soon joined the armed forces. Their military experiences are indicated above.

The 1930's were marked by aggressive acts by Japan, Italy, and Germany that led to the cataclysm of World War II. During the decade, Japan invaded Manchuria and China, Italy's Benito Mussolini subdued Ethiopia, and Nazi Germany's Adolf Hitler seized the Rhineland, Austria, and Czechoslovakia. (Finding the Boy Scout movement incompatible with Nazi ideology, Germany dissolved its Scout association in 1934, replacing it with the militaristic Hitler Youth. Earlier, in 1924, another totalitarian state, the Soviet Union, banned its Boy Scout association and organized the Young Pioneers to perpetuate its Communist ideals.)

On September 1, 1939, German troops smashed into Poland. Two days later Great Britain and France declared war on Germany.

Until the invasion of Poland, the United States had pursued a policy of hopeful neutrality. Isolationist sentiment ran high. After the Nazi blitzkrieg in Poland, the United States remained officially neutral, but there was a decided tilt toward the Allies—Britain, France, and later the Soviet Union. Preparedness became the American watchword. During the next 2 years, production of war materials was stepped up, defense plants were built, and a draft was instituted to beef up America's armed forces.

The Boy Scouts of America joined in the preparedness effort. In 1940 a plan for cooperation with the federal Office of Civilian Defense was approved and an emergency service training program got under way. Out of this grew the Emergency Service Corps made up of older Boy Scouts who had full training in first aid and service during disasters.

In the summer of 1941, at the request of President Roosevelt, Boy Scouts and Cub Scouts placed 1.6 million posters in retail stores, advertising the

I REMEMBER . . .

The Scene: *Old Colony Council in Massachusetts during World War II*

In this area we had a very active Civilian Defense group and air raid precautions operation. They decided to put on a huge air raid drill and asked the Boy Scouts to provide "victims." Presumably Fall River had been bombed. The victims were precisely placed around the area with tags indicating that this person was dead, this person had a broken left leg, and so on. I was in the control office after the drill was over, and everybody had reported in except one Scout. The missing boy was the one who was to be at the corner of Washington Street. So we went there, and there was no boy. We were near a church, and hanging on the iron railing of the church was the tag that should have been around the boy's neck. The tag said "Arterial bleeding of the left leg." And underneath it the kid had written, "I have bled to death and gone home." —*Rod Speirs*

government's Defense bonds and stamps. Scouts in 11,369 communities collected nearly 5,000 tons of aluminum scrap, mostly pots and pans, for recycling into war planes. Scouts also gathered huge quantitites of wastepaper for recycling to relieve a paper shortage.

That December, after the Japanese attack on Pearl Harbor, the Boy Scouts of America redoubled its efforts. During the 4 years of American involvement in World War II, Scouting's major home-front services were the collection of scrap materials, distribution of posters and pamphlets, and growing food. Cub Scouts shared in these campaigns with their older brothers.

The BSA was not called upon to take pledges for the U.S. Treasury's War Bonds and Savings Stamps, as they had in World War I, but they delivered millions of War Bond pledge cards, and it was estimated that they were indirectly responsible for sales of $1.8 million worth of bonds and stamps.

Periodic waste collection drives were held throughout the war. The totals collected by Boy Scouts and Cub Scouts are awesome: 5,898 tons of rubber, primarily old tires; 17,400 tons of tin cans; and 20,800 tons of other scrap metals. Recyclable rubber was essential for war production because there were few synthetic substitutes and the raw rubber supply was cut off by war in the Far East. All types of metals were also vital to make the war materiel for our own armed forces and for America's role as the "arsenal of democracy" for all the Allies.

In 1944, Boy Scouts were sent into the woods to collect milkweed floss as a substitute for the kapok used in life jackets. Their total: 750 tons. The

Above, a Memphis, Tenn., Scout exhibits 1,657 keys he collected during a national metal-salvage drive; right, the mayor of Auburn, N. Y., pitches in.

largest single war-service project, however, was the Gen. Dwight D. Eisenhower Waste Paper campaign in the spring of 1945. More than 700,000 Boy Scouts and Cub Scouts gathered 318,000 tons of paper, bringing the total paper collection during the war years to 591,000 tons. In one waste-paper drive, in 1942, Scouts overwhelmed storage facilities with 150,000 tons, and the War Production Board begged them to stop their "magnificent job."

Not everything they gathered was scrap. Scouts collected 10 million used books for servicemen and, as the war neared its end, 7,000 tons of used clothing for distribution to refugees in Europe and China.

Hundreds of thousands of Scouts augmented the nation's food supply with Victory Gardens. The total number is unknown, but in 1944, as the tide of victory was flowing toward the Allies, an estimated 184,000 Scouts had gardens. In addition, 126,000 Boy Scouts helped farmers with their harvests. Some councils operated work camps from which Boy Scouts fanned out each day to aid shorthanded farmers.

Boy Scouts were assigned as messengers for Civilian Defense air raid wardens and control centers, and at hospitals, fire stations, and police precinct houses. Others were given the title of Dispatch Bearer and went door to door delivering millions of pamphlets on the war effort.

The Emergency Service Corps became an important auxiliary for vital services in many communities. Typical of the Corps' work was the organization in Palisades Park, N.J., across the Hudson River from New York City. Herbert R. Bieri, a Scoutmaster and neighborhood commissioner, organized a force of 27 older Scouts from the town's five troops.

"We assigned the boys to the fire department, the ambulance corps, the Civilian Defense air-ground observation group, and the police," Bieri recalled. "Each of these groups trained the boys assigned to them. During a blackout the boys would put on their special armbands—there was no time to put on a uniform—and respond to the unit they were trained to work with."

In some cities, Civilian Defense workers visited troops to give special training. Raul Chavez, who was a Scout in Los Angeles during the early years of the war, remembered that demonstrations were given in such wartime skills as how to extinguish an incendiary bomb with a shovel and bucket of sand.

One Boy Scout used his Scoutcraft training to aid in the capture of two German saboteurs. Scout Harvard M. Hodgkins, 17, of Hancock Point, Me., was driving home on the night of November 29, 1944, when he spotted two men walking through the snowy woods. He noted that they were wearing lightweight coats, which no Down Easter would have on in late November. Hodgkins got out of the car and backtracked their footprints to the seashore. Guessing correctly that the two men had been put ashore by submarine, Hodgkins notified the FBI, which quickly apprehended them. The Scout's alert action earned him a red-carpet reception in New York City.

There was less military flavor in Boy Scout activities than there had been during World War I when many people, including Scoutmasters, still thought of Scouting as a semimilitary movement. Turnover among Scoutmasters and Cubmasters was rapid; more than half of all Scoutmasters were in the armed forces by 1945. But willing replacements were found for most of them, and Scouting's membership continued to rise throughout the war.

Thousands of Senior Scouts and Sea Scouts went off to war with their leaders. Sea Scouts and skippers were especially prized by the Navy and Coast Guard for their seamanship training, and by the end of 1943 some 75,000 former Sea Scouts were serving, many as commissioned officers. Among them was Commander Thomas J. Keane, who had joined the BSA's

An emergency trailer made by Scouts in Springfield, Mass., in 1941, spreads the patriotic word.

Denver Scouts—still wearing knickers—haul scrap metal in a converted motorcycle sidecar.

professional ranks after a career in the Navy and built Sea Scouting to a membership of 25,000 boys and men.

Since 1936 Keane had headed the Senior Scouting Service, which included all programs for older boys—Senior Scouting in the troop, Sea Scouting, Explorer Scouting, Rovering, the Order of the Arrow, the Knights of Dunamis (an organization of Eagle Scouts), and smaller organizations called troop alumni, press club, and senior honor society. In 1942, still another program was added—Air Scouting for boys 15 and older.

Air Scouts did not learn to pilot a plane and were not supposed to fly even as passengers, but probably some had rides with their squadron advisers. (In 1946, flying, but not pilot training, was approved for Air Scouts.) They learned navigation, aerodynamics, and some of the skills needed to repair airplane engines. As part of their training, Air Scouts also built model planes, and about 100,000 of them were given to the Army Air Corps for training pilots and air observers.

Among the first Air Scout squadrons was one at the naval air base at Pensacola, Fla. The adviser was Navy pilot Alan N. Lobeck, who achieved the top ranks in three Scouting programs—Eagle Scout, Sea Scout Quartermaster, and Air Scout Ace. He remembered, "We had about 60 boys in the squadron. A lot of them were interested in flying, and we lost them because learning to fly was not part of the regular program. They left and went to the Civil Air Patrol so they could actually fly." Even so, Air Scouting grew rapidly during the war. At the end of 1944 more than 11,000 boys and men were enrolled.

The Boy Scouts of America was still seeking a unified program to cover the varying interests of young men. In 1945, Senior Scouting in the troop

Albuquerque Scouts harvest a bushel of beans from their victory garden to take to a local day nursery.

was discontinued, and the BSA began studying methods to meet the needs and desires of all older boys. The following year unification of the three main offerings—Explorer Scouting, Sea Scouting, and Air Scouting—moved a step closer with the adoption of a single work uniform for the 69,000 young men in all three branches. But it would be several more years before they would merge into a new Exploring program.

The Boy Scouts of America, in spite of local segregation practices, made slow but steady progress in bringing blacks into its programs during the late 1930's and the war years. By 1944 more than 100,000 black boys and men were in Scouting and all local councils had approved their entry, although blacks were still barred in some districts within a few councils.

In many councils, there were restrictions on blacks wearing the uniform even in the 1940's, said Frank Dix, a professional Scouter who worked in the BSA's regional office in Atlanta from 1943 to 1948. "There were some councils where statements were made officially by the executive board that when the first black boy appears in uniform we will take all our Boy Scout handbooks down to the city square and burn them," Dix recalled. In some areas, black Scouts could buy the uniform only after earning either Second or First Class rank.

Nearly every council in the South had camps for black Scouts, but they were sadly lacking in facilities. Dix, a white native of the Deep South, remembered, "I inspected most of the camps as a member of the regional staff, and they were very, very pitiful operations."

Dix pointed out that black Scouts were not universally welcomed in the North, either. "It would create the wrong impression if it were implied that all the racial problems existed in the South only." Dix said that in

Scouts hold one of many War Bond rallies around the nation, at the Federal Hall National Memorial, in New York City.

New Jersey Scouts invite their neighbors to "pan Hitler."

1948 when he went to the Chicago Council as director of field operations, one of his first jobs was to integrate the council. At the time, Chicago, like many other northern communities, maintained a separate district called a division for blacks, just as Charleston, S.C., and other southern councils did. "I was threatened by an alderman," he said. "In fact, I had more threats in Chicago than I did in Atlanta."

The World War II era saw the severing of the last links with Scouting's infancy in America. National Scout Commissioner Daniel Carter Beard died in Suffern, N.Y., on June 11, 1941, 10 days before his 91st birthday, and Chief Scout Executive James E. West retired at the end of 1943.

For a generation, Uncle Dan Beard had personified Scouting and James E. West had been its guardian. Louis A. Hornbeck, who was Scout executive in Suffern during Dan Beard's final years, put it this way: "It was very much like Dan Beard was the King of England with James E. West as prime minister."

For most of his 30 years in Scouting, Beard had been the best known and beloved figure in the movement. He was a frequent contributor to *Boys' Life* and chairman of the national Court of Honor, which awarded medals for lifesaving and meritorious service. He also led thousands of Boy Scouts on an annual pilgrimage to the grave of President Theodore Roosevelt, an early advocate of Scouting, in Oyster Bay, N.Y.

James E. West retired full of honors and the knowledge that he was chiefly responsible for the firm foundations and high repute of the Boy Scouts of America. He could claim the lion's share of credit for its organizational structures from the troop committee to the national office. West lacked the charismatic appeal to boys of Dan Beard or Ernest Thompson Seton, but his commitment to youth was no less strong than theirs. His constant message was: "We must never forget that our main purpose first, last and all the time is to create and maintain conditions so that boys intensely desire to become Scouts, and men of character are willing to give leadership." West died on May 15, 1948, the eve of his 72nd birthday.

To succeed him as Chief Scout Executive, the national Executive Board chose one of its own. He was Dr. Elbert K. Fretwell, a recently retired professor of education at Columbia University's Teachers College.

The Good Turn Tradition

The BSA's 1913 annual report bore this sentimental frontispiece.

An early exhortative poster.

Origins of a Grand Ideal

"Every Boy Scout must do at least one good turn to somebody every day," early Scout literature stated. The most celebrated Good Turn of all was one of the first, when in 1910 an anonymous British lad refused a tip after leading Chicago publisher W. D. Boyce to his destination in fogbound London. The boy explained that "I am a Scout. I can't take anything for helping"; the much-impressed Boyce later reciprocated by endowing the BSA. Since then, "Do a Good Turn Daily" has been the official Scout slogan, and millions of Scouts have strived to make selfless, generous behavior a part of their everyday lives.

The incident of the unknown Scout is recreated in this airbrush painting by Donald N. Ross.

147

Above, a Scout leader holds onto a bottle-feeding baby bear.

Opposite, a Cub brings a cow into focus.

Below, a young Scout cuddles a tamed beaver.

Caring for Animals, Too

Photos of Scouts with innocent beasts were staples of local papers all across the country in the middle part of the century. The pictures were usually sweet but undramatic; behind them, however, lies a Scout tradition of courage and skill in dealing with animals. The BSA's National Court of Honor grants certificates for heroism and medals for bold action every year, and they often involve animals. From the 1978 report: "On January 22 . . . Steven Andregg, 8, was hiking on the family farm near Ft. Gibson, Okla., when the Andreggs' dog ran out on the ice on Manard Bayou and fell through. His older companions, brother Mark Andregg and Scout Mike Nelson, both 11, began looking for rocks to throw on the ice to break a channel for the dog, but young Steven walked out onto the ice and fell through into 5-foot-deep water. Remembering his Scout training in ice rescues, Mike quickly attached a long-strapped canteen to his coat, threw it to Steven and pulled him to safety. Mike's coolness and alertness saved Steven's life and was in Scouting's best traditions." His actions, it might be added, demonstrated concern for an animal's welfare as well as preparedness to save a human life.

A Scout accompanies two elderly veterans at the 1913 Gettysburg reunion.

A small girl and her wagon merit full attention from this Scout.

Good Turns for Young and Old

When thousands of aged Civil War veterans gathered at Gettysburg in 1913 for the fiftieth anniversary of the great battle there, 548 Boy Scouts gathered too, to help care for them. Good Turns for the elderly, as well as for the very young, were already a part of Scout life. *American Boy* magazine reported a typical experience in New Jersey in 1912: "One lad saw a veteran walking up and down in front of his father's store and took a chair out to him, asking him to sit down and wait until the car he wanted came along. He told him he was a Scout. The same lad pulled a younger boy from in front of a horse and wagon which were coming along at a swift pace, thereby saving the boy from certain injury."

At left, an Atlanta Scout returns a lost child to its home; above, New York City Scouts help the police department provide Christmas gifts for the needy.

In the three pictures at right, Boy Scouts help control crowds at the inauguration of President Woodrow Wilson in 1913.

A Chivalric Code

Sir Robert Baden-Powell drew many of his ideals for Scouts' behavior from the ethical standards of medieval knights, and even developed the Scout motto ("Be prepared") and law from an old chivalric code: "Be always ready with your armor on, except when you are taking rest at night. Defend the poor, and help them that cannot help themselves. Do nothing to hurt or offend anyone else. Be prepared to fight in the defense of your country. At whatever you are working, try to win honor and a name for honesty. Never break your promise. Maintain the honor of your country with your life. Rather die honest than live shamelessly. Chivalry requireth that you should be trained to perform the most laborious and humble offices with cheerfulness and grace, and do good unto others."

Coach Fielding Yost, of the University of Michigan, turns out with his whole team to buy a war bond from Scouts, 1917.

153

Depression-era Scouts load provisions onto a truck bound for a Red Cross emergency warehouse.

New signs are posted along the main thoroughfare of an unidentified town—it could be almost anywhere in the country.

Scouts in Beaumont, Tex., make a traffic count of cars traveling to and from local defense plants during World War II.

The Daughters of the American Revolution honor Scouts for their help in New York in 1936.

Helping the Community

Boys' Life reported in 1922 that "Good turns go on turning merrily all over the country," and took particular notice of acts of everyday helpfulness to local communities. "Dallas, Texas, Scouts delivered over 25,000 bulletins for the City Fair Association. Ruthton, Minn., Scouts cleaned all the gutters along Main Street. Provo, Utah, Scouts made a collection of loose rocks and stones extracted from the roads. Demig, New Mexico, Scouts picked up 192 pounds of nails and 61 pounds of glass from the city streets." These deeds recall another historic ideal built into Scouting by Baden-Powell, the Oath of the Young Man of Athens. It appears in the *Boy Scout Handbook* as follows: "We will never bring disgrace on this our City, by an act of dishonesty or cowardice. We will fight for the ideals and Sacred Things of the City both alone and with many. We will revere and obey the City's laws, and will do our best to incite a like reverence and respect in those above us who are prone to annul them or set them at naught. We will strive increasingly to quicken the public's sense of civic duty. Thus in all these ways we will transmit this City, not only not less, but greater and more beautiful than it was transmitted to us." Centuries later, the Boy Scouts of America follow the precepts of that pledge in their own towns and cities.

A Massachusetts Scout posts a public warning.

Ready for All Emergencies

More than 5,000 teenagers nationwide learn invaluable emergency skills by taking part in fire Exploring. They are instructed in how to use and maintain professional firefighting equipment and study the crucial rules and procedures that firemen must follow. Many of them go on to careers with local fire departments. Since safety is paramount, these Explorers have strict limitations on their activities. They may never fight actual fires, enter burning buildings, or drive the big trucks. They help in countless ways behind the scenes, though, and engage in exciting and lifelike practice courses, as shown in the photographs on these two pages.

Above, an Explorer in Phoenix, Arizona, prepares to enter an often-burning building used to train firemen. Below, another Explorer gets used to wearing oxygen equipment. Opposite, an Explorer discovers the strength needed to haul a hose.

Painting the church is a job for the whole troop working together.

Atop a high ladder, a Scout scrubs clean a church window.

Serving the Chartered Organization

Many Scout troops engage in special Good Turn programs that help out their chartered organizations—the churches, synagogues, schools, and other groups that sponsor them. In East Brunswick and New Brunswick, N. J., the Scouts shown on these pages participate regularly in their chartered organizations' clean-up programs and worship services. It's a much appreciated way of saying thank you to the organizing group behind the troop, and it gives the Scouts a special, useful way of getting involved in the activities of their local place of worship.

A Scout studies the Torah with his rabbi.

6
Reaching the Heights

Americans everywhere must be proud to know that the Boy Scouts of America registered its 3,000,000th active member during the past year. . . . This BSA birthday message is addressed to every Scout and leader in the Boy Scouts of America. I urge you all to live up to the high ideals for which Scouting stands—your duty as patriotic citizens. If you will follow the Scout Oath America will be better able to meet its full responsibility in cooperation with other nations in maintaining peace on earth.
— President Dwight D. Eisenhower, February 8, 1953

THE POST–WORLD WAR II ERA was a golden age for the Boy Scouts of America. Millions of former GI's were marrying and starting families, and by the mid-1950's when their first sons were reaching Cub Scout age, the BSA was recording membership gains of 200,000 or more a year.

It was a time of constantly rising living standards—more single-family homes, more cars, more household appliances, more leisure time. The postwar period was marked, too, by the Cold War with our erstwhile ally, the Soviet Union, a hot war in Korea, and by a Red scare fostered by Senator Joseph McCarthy, whose charges of Communists in government set American against American. The Boy Scouts of America avoided entanglements in the political realm, but patriotic feeling was fervid. The Cold War and its effects were reflected in continuing emphasis on respect for

Cub Scouts greet President Eisenhower in Thomasville, Ga., in 1956.

Norman Rockwell created this Scout for the cover of the new Handbook *that appeared in 1960.*

161

Tennessee Scouts in the late 1940's show off a wood-and-rope bridge they just finished constructing.

flag and country and by continuing cooperation with the postwar Department of Civil Defense. The titles of two BSA national programs— "Crusade to Strengthen the Arm of Liberty" and "Forward on Liberty's Team"— suggest the tenor of the times.

The war had finished isolationism in America, and through the Marshall Plan the United States helped to rebuild the shattered economies of western Europe. The Boy Scouts of America had its own "Marshall Plan." Called the World Friendship Fund, it was started in 1944 with contributions from American Scouts and Scouters to aid struggling Scout associations in war-torn nations. Over the past 4 decades, three-quarters of a million dollars has been given to the fund; today it is used to provide training, uniforms, and equipment to Scout associations in the underdeveloped world.

American families were increasingly child-centered after the war, and so parental involvement in Scouting was strong. By today's standards, volunteer leaders were a dime a dozen; many packs and troops had auxiliaries of parents, usually mothers, in addition to the regular unit committee.

Scouts were widely respected by their peers. Some youths might sneer at "Boy Sprouts" and call them "sissies" (a phenomenon that was noted as early as the 1920's) but most non-Scouts were admiring, or at worst indifferent, to Scouting. Peer pressure pushed boys toward Scouting rather than away from it.

The baby boom, the broad public approval of Scouting, and the standing of the BSA as a bulwark of patriotism all played a part in the steadily climbing membership statistics. So did the decisive, imaginative leadership of Arthur A. Schuck, who succeeded Elbert K. Fretwell as Chief Scout Executive in 1948. Schuck was the first Chief with professional Scouting experience; he had been a council and regional executive and national head of field operations. Another important factor was the lowering of minimum entry ages for the BSA's three programs—Cub Scouting, Boy Scouting, and Exploring—in 1949. The entry age for Cub Scouts was dropped to 8, for Boy Scouts to 11, and for Explorers to 14.

At the end of the war, total registration in the BSA was just under 2 million. In the first 3 postwar years, annual increases were 70,000 to 85,000. With the new age limits in place in 1949, the membership jumped by 369,000. The peak membership year, though, came in 1954 when the first boys in the baby boom were turning 8 years of age and the BSA's registration total went up by 378,131. Membership topped 3 million in 1952, 4 million 3 years later, 5 million in 1959, and 6 million in 1967.

All three programs shared in the rapid growth, with Cub Scouting leading the way. By the early fifties, Cub Scouting had overtaken its big brother, Boy Scouting. In part, though, Cub Scouting's preeminence was due to a change in the basis of compiling statistics because in 1949 all Boy Scouts 14 and older were counted as Explorers.

That change came with the announcement of a unified Exploring program. All three special sections for older boys—Explorer Scouting, Sea Scouting, and Air Scouting—were grouped under the title of Exploring; the members henceforth would be known as just plain Explorers, Sea Explorers, and Air Explorers, depending on their specialties. For Sea and Air Explorers, the change was a matter of title, not substance.

For the old Senior Scouts and Explorer Scouts there were substantive changes. Boys could remain in a Scout troop after their 14th birthday but they would be registered as Explorers—not Explorer Scouts. They could wear either the Boy Scout uniform or the new green Explorer uniform.

Twenty-six Tennessee Scouts pose for their picture after winning their Eagle badges in the 1950's.

(Boy Scouts were no longer wearing breeches after the war; trousers and an overseas-style cap became official in 1943; long pants were authorized for Cub Scouts in 1947.)

Older boys in Scout troops were given two options. They could remain in the troop as members of an Explorer crew, or they could join a separate unit for Explorers called a post. Explorer crews in troops had their own adult leaders called Advisors. They took part in troop meetings and held special activities of their own such as rugged backpacking trips, canoeing expeditions, and perhaps an occasional party or dance to which Senior Girl Scouts or Campfire Girls were invited. Explorers could continue through Boy Scouting's ranks or follow a new Exploring advancement plan.

The position of Explorer Advisor in a troop was somewhat ambiguous; he was coequal with the Scoutmaster but led only what amounted to a senior patrol. Walter K. Josti, a Scoutmaster in Worcester, Mass., took over as crew Advisor when Exploring was introduced into his Troop 84. Because he was also a roundtable commissioner, Josti saw the plan in action in other troops, and, he said, "In some troops the Scoutmaster and Advisor bumped heads all the time. If one was stronger than the other or they weren't cooperating, you had conflicting interests." That wasn't a problem in every troop, though. Leighton (Andy) Parezo, who was an Explorer Advisor in Troop 97 in Washington, D.C., remembered no conflict: "I went along on all troop activities as if I was an assistant Scoutmaster."

Walter Josti said his Explorer crew did some vocational exploration, visiting industries and bringing in experts in various fields. Both Josti and Parezo recalled social activities, too—training in the social graces and well-chaperoned parties and cookouts with girls. Both also said their Explorer crews hiked, camped, and took trips apart from their troops. "But," Josti said, "we tried to keep the Explorers from being too distinctive; they were like the leadership corps is now in a troop."

In a few troops, Exploring was ignored. "We didn't pay any attention to it," said Scoutmaster Norman A. Greist of Troop 1, Hamden, Conn. "We had our own program for older boys. We registered them as Boy Scouts, and they were very much a part of the troop." Once a month the older

Walt Disney presents

Follow Me, Boys!

Scoutmaster Fred MacMurray and his charges watch as their homemade clubhouse collapses in the 1966 Disney movie Follow Me, Boys!

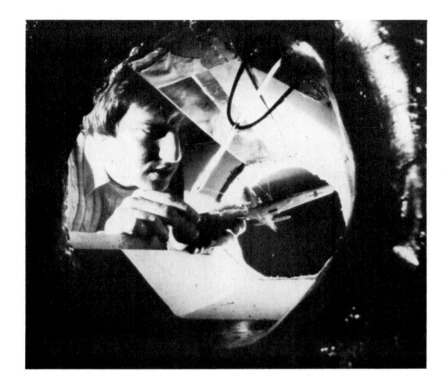

An Explorer interested in aviation learns first-hand about aerodynamics and wind-tunnel research techniques.

Scouts had a special event, he said, but they remained an integral part of the troop.

This mishmash of arrangements—with some Explorers in troops, others in posts, and still other older boys continuing as Boy Scouts—went on for a decade. It ended in 1959 when today's Exploring program was born. Sea Exploring and Air Exploring were unchanged, but boys 14 and older who wanted to remain in Scout troops were again called Boy Scouts. All others became Explorers in separate posts.

The main innovation of the new Exploring program was provision for "special-interest" or "career-interest" Explorer posts whose activities centered on careers or avocations instead of on advanced Scouting skills. Special-interest Exploring grew out of a 1954 University of Michigan study which found that more than four out of five high school–age youths were concerned about adult careers and were eager to explore the possibilities.

The first special-interest posts were organized in California in 1956 by William H. Spurgeon III, a businessman and National Exploring Committee member who became the chief advocate of specialized Exploring. He spent 3 years stumping the country to spread the word about the appeal of the program, not just for older Scouts but for all high school–age youth.

Special-interest posts soon appeared in all parts of the country with such specialties as astronautics, medicine, law, auto mechanics, merchandising, banking, science, conservation, and forestry. As a result, the range of sponsors for Explorer posts broadened considerably beyond the churches, schools, and civic organizations which had always been (and continue to be) the prime sources of sponsorship for Scouting units. Businesses,

I REMEMBER . . .

The Scene: *Reading, Pa., 1950–60*

Oh, it was a great time for Scouting! It was a time when a lot of parents still remembered the Depression, and they weren't handing everything to boys. We could take boys to our troop's camp for $5 or $6 a week. At that time our council didn't have a camp, but when the council camp started it only cost about $25 a week.

Gradually we became a little more sophisticated, but the boys didn't demand as much and they seemed to have more fun with simple things than they do now. We had a beautiful stream that ran through our camp, and I never tried to keep kids out of it because it was a great thing to build a dam and catch salamanders and frogs. Today if a kid gets wet, his mother says, "My kid came home all muddy. What's the big idea?" It didn't seem to bother mothers as much in those days.

—*Richard F. Kurr*

industries, labor unions, hospitals, trade associations, and other nontraditional sponsors backed career-interest posts.

For some years the majority of Explorer posts continued as advanced Scouting units, but career-interest Exploring made steady inroads. Today 90 percent of all Explorer posts concentrate on careers or other special interests.

In 1969, a decade after the new Exploring program began, another significant step was taken: girls were permitted to become "participants" in special-interest Explorer posts, but were not registered. Two years later girls were allowed to register as Explorers.

The Cub Scouting and Boy Scouting programs were changing, too, during the postwar period, although less drastically than Exploring. In 1947 advancement requirements were revised for both programs, but there was no change in emphasis. Cub Scouts still progressed from Wolf to Bear to Lion with roughly similar subject matter for each rank, and Cub Scouting remained home- and neighborhood-centered. Boy Scout tests continued to stress Scoutcraft and outdoor skills.

In Cub Scouting the dropout rate was high, apparently because of the lack of variety on the way to the Lion badge and graduation into Boy Scouting. In 1954 Lion Cub Scouts were put into a separate unit called the Webelos den when they reached the age of 10½, but they were given no new challenges. (Webelos is an acronym for "We'll be loyal Scouts.") Four years later, Webelos den leaders were given suggested activities to keep these older Cub Scouts interested until their 11th birthday and graduation into Boy Scouting.

These minor changes failed to stem the dropout tide, so in 1967 the whole Cub Scout advancement plan was revised. The Lion rank was dropped, and the 10-year-olds, now called Webelos Scouts, were given an entirely new program under male leadership. The heart of Webelos Scouting was 15 activity badges for work in such career fields as engineering and geology and such avocations as sports and aquatics. As preparation for Boy Scouting, Webelos Scouts were to have one or two overnight campouts with their fathers. Requirements for the Wolf and Bear badges were revamped, too, with entirely different advancement subjects for each year. The minimum age for Cub Scouts was relaxed slightly; all third-grade boys could join Cub Scouting, even if they were not yet 8 years old.

The post-World War II era was the heyday of highly visible national Good Turns which sent millions of Cub Scouts, Boy Scouts, and Explorers into action. At intervals of about 2 years, the Boy Scouts of America called on its members for national service.

In late 1950 and early 1951, 2 million pounds of clothing were collected for overseas relief at the request of the American Council of Voluntary Agencies for Foreign Service and the United Nations. In 1952, 1.8 million boys went house to house and business to business placing 30 million "Liberty Bell" doorknob hangers and a million posters to remind citizens to vote in the presidential election. Two years later, in the spring and summer of 1954, a national conservation Good Turn sent millions into the streets and backwoods of the country. They distributed 3.6 million copies of a conservation poster. In the nation's parks, rural areas, and wildernesses, Scouts undertook a host of conservation projects: 6.2 million trees were planted, 55,000 bird nesting boxes were built and set out, 41,000 conservation exhibits were placed on public display, and packs, troops, and posts tackled thousands of others projects to control erosion, improve the nation's forests and wildlife habitats, and educate their fellow citizens on the need for conservation of natural resources.

In 1956, the BSA's members again went door to door in an impressive get-out-the-vote campaign. Some 36 million doorknob hangers and 1.35 million posters were distributed. Virtually every pack, troop, and post in the nation took part; in terms of participation, it was the largest Good Turn in Scouting's history.

The 1958 national Good Turn focused on safety. Forty million emergency handbooks prepared by the Office of Civil Defense Mobilization were delivered to the nation's households and 50,000 posters were placed in post offices. The safety message was also imprinted on milk cartons and emblazoned on 1,500 billboards.

Two years later another get-out-the-vote drive was the service feature. It was the last national Good Turn until the beginning of a conservation campaign called Project SOAR (Save Our American Resources) in 1970.

The quarter-century after World War II also saw development of national jamborees into extravaganzas of Scouting. Although only a small percentage of Boy Scouts and Explorers were able to attend jamborees (Cub Scouts were not eligible), the excitement of preparation and the spectacular scope of the encampments themselves breathed renewed vigor into the whole organization.

The second national jamboree was held at Valley Forge, Pa., in 1950 and attracted 47,000 boys and leaders from every state and territory and several other countries. Over the next 2 decades, national jamborees were

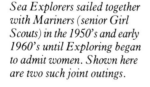

Sea Explorers sailed together with Mariners (senior Girl Scouts) in the 1950's and early 1960's until Exploring began to admit women. Shown here are two such joint outings.

held at Irvine Ranch in southern California in 1953, with 45,000 participants; 1957 at Valley Forge again, with 50,000; 1960 at Colorado Springs, Colo., 56,000; 1964 at Valley Forge for the third time, 52,000; and 1969 at Farragut State Park, Idaho, 35,000.

Between the sixth and seventh national jamborees, the Boy Scouts of America were host to their first world jamboree. It was held in 1967 at Farragut State Park and drew 12,000 Scouts and leaders from 107 countries; about half were from the United States. (Eleven previous world jamborees had been held in England, Denmark, Hungary, Holland, France, Austria, Canada, the Philippines, and Greece; the BSA was represented at all of them by small delegations.)

For older Boy Scouts and Explorers who could not go to a jamboree, the BSA was offering an excellent alternative—a week or two at Philmont Scout Ranch at Cimarron, N. Mex. The 36,000-acre nucleus of Philmont, which now covers 137,000 acres of wild country in northern New Mexico, was given to the Boy Scouts of America in 1938 by Waite Phillips, a Tulsa, Okla., oilman and philanthropist. Three years later Phillips gave an additional 91,000 acres and the 23-story Philtower Building in Tulsa to provide income for an endowment for the ranch.

Philmont offered backpacking, horseback riding, mountain climbing, and other outdoor adventures for Scouts and Explorers and was soon drawing boys from every part of the country. The number of Philmont campers grew steadily, from about 1,600 in the years immediately after the war to 17,000 in the mid-1960's. By that time, training courses were being held at Philmont for Scouters, both volunteers and professionals, and many took their families along on a busman's holiday.

I REMEMBER . . .

The Scene: *Westchester County, N.Y., 1950–65*

In those days it was *the* thing to be in Scouting. In Scarsdale, for instance, because of the way the school districts were laid out, we showed 105 percent of the boys who were eligible to be Cub Scouts and Boy Scouts as registered in Scouting. Virtually all of the Scarsdale boys were in Scouting, and we also had boys who lived in neighboring communities but went to school in Scarsdale and joined Scouting there.

Scarsdale is a very sophisticated town of wealth, and of course the high school is a very sophisticated operation, but it was Eagle Scouts in uniform who ran all the flag ceremonies at school assembly programs. Scouting and its uniform were an integral part of Scarsdale. That's changed. We still have packs and troops in Scarsdale, but Scouting hasn't the strong image it had in those years.

—Joe Cooke

Back home in the local councils, Scout camping was changing. In the BSA's infancy and adolescence, when Boy Scouts attended the council summer camp they went as individuals, not with their troops. Loose-knit patrols of boys from several communities might be formed for Scoutcraft and games in camp. Gradually this system evolved into a formal patrol and troop structure for camp, but Scouts still came as individuals. By the end of the war, whole troops were attending summer camp together in the pattern that prevails today.

Council camp facilities and leadership were being upgraded. National camping schools were held in each of the BSA's 12 regions to train camp directors, activities specialists, and commissary officers. Council camps found a bonanza in military surplus goods after the war. They got cots, tents, kitchen equipment, chlorinating systems and pumps and engines for the asking or at bargain-basement prices. Some councils also picked up sleeping bags, cook kits, and tents for sale at low prices to Scouts and troops.

In the late 1960's nearly 800,000 Scouts, representing 65 percent of all troops, were attending summer camp each year. They had it easier than their fathers did. Scouts were less likely to hike than to camp; when they did hike, their loads were lighter. Jack V. Howard, a Scoutmaster in Sacramento, Calif., during the fifties, remembered, "When I was a Boy Scout in 1926, if you went camping 100 miles from home, that was a heck of a long trip so most of your camping was close by. Beginning in the fifties, 100 miles was just a jaunt." Howard continued, "And in the fifties, new equipment became available—lighter tents and down sleeping bags.

Astronaut Walter Schirra receives a special one-of-a-kind Astronaut Merit Badge in October 1962, just after his six-orbit space mission in the Mercury capsule Sigma 7.

And then there was the coming of dehydrated foods and ready-mixes. Back in the early days you had to carry your own baking powder, baking soda and flour and so on, and those ingredients had to be mixed to make something. But in the fifties, you had Bisquick and that kind of thing. It made camping a lot easier.''

Did it make Scouting better? "Well," said Howard, "you've got to go with the times. I don't know whether it made it better but it made it easier.''

In the wake of Scouting's soaring membership gains, *Boys' Life* magazine enjoyed unparalleled prosperity. By the late sixties, *Boys' Life* had 2.65 million subscribers, including 350,000 non-Scouts, and was the 17th biggest magazine in the United States.

It was a far cry from 1912 when the Boy Scouts of America took over the monthly magazine and began publishing it for 6,000 boys. In the intervening years, two generations of boys had grown up waiting impatiently by their mailboxes for *their* magazine; for hundreds of thousands, it was their only mail.

Boys' Life had published such famous authors as Rudyard Kipling, O. Henry, Zane Grey, Pearl S. Buck, Jack London, P. G. Wodehouse, and William Saroyan. Stories of true-life adventure and inspirational messages had come from Orville Wright, Charles Lindbergh, Joe Louis, Admiral Richard E. Byrd, and Connie Mack. Readers had learned Scoutcraft and the thrills of outdoor life from Dan Beard, Ernest Thompson Seton, and Theodore Roosevelt. For 2 years during its infancy, *Boys' Life* had featured the drawings and paintings of Norman Rockwell, who was later to earn renown for his covers for the *Saturday Evening Post*, the behemoth of magazines during the first half of the century. Rockwell also painted an idealized world of Scouting for the annual calendars of Brown & Bigelow.

On the strength of its ties with the Boy Scouts of America, *Boys' Life* outlasted all competition. At its birth several magazines were competing for youthful readers. *Youth's Companion* succumbed in 1929, *St. Nicholas* in 1943, and *American Boy* and *Open Road* in 1954.

Boys' Life survived and prospered as the BSA prospered. Each month its faithful readers laughed at the jokes on the "Think & Grin" page, devoured the tales of heroism in "Scouts in Action," tried their hand at the magazine's how-to and Scoutcraft ideas, and avidly consumed the stories of adventure, sports heroes, and mysteries in its articles and fiction.

The face of America and American society was changing fast in the postwar period. Millions of newly affluent workers left the big cities to find the good life in the suburbs. Sleepy villages ringing the metropolises were transformed into bustling communities of upwardly mobile former city dwellers; the cities increasingly became havens for the poor and the very rich.

At the same time, the civil rights revolution triggered by the Supreme Court's *Brown* v. *Board of Education* decision was creating rising expectations among blacks and other minorities. Sit-ins, freedom rides, and demonstrations in the South upset the social patterns of a century. In the late sixties, riots ripped several cities with large black populations. There was unrest, too, in colleges and universities over demands for student power and protests against America's escalating involvement in the Vietnam War. The assassinations of President John F. Kennedy, his brother Robert, and civil rights leader Martin Luther King, Jr., during the 1960's were symptomatic of the growing divisions in American society.

The social changes brought new challenges to the Boy Scouts of America. It became more difficult to organize Cub Scout packs, Boy Scout troops, and Explorer posts in the inner cities. Adult volunteers, the backbone of the Scouting movement, were hard to recruit among the poor, and money for uniforms and equipment was in short supply. Family ties were weaker than they had been in Scouting's early years, and the young were less respectful of parents, teachers, and such other authority figures as Scout leaders.

To meet what was perceived to be a major challenge—how to bring Scouting to poor boys in the inner city and depressed rural areas—the BSA began an Inner-City Rural Program in 1965. Led by Chief Scout Executive Joseph A. Brunton, Jr., who had succeeded Arthur A. Schuck in 1960, the Inner-City Rural Program was the largest research and development effort ever undertaken by the Boy Scouts of America.

Its aim was to identify and learn how to overcome obstacles to Scouting in low-income areas. For 6 years special projects testing various approaches were operated and closely monitored in 18 inner cities and rural areas. Some traditional methods of organizing went by the boards. Store-front Scout centers manned by professionals were opened in several cities. An aggressive campaign to form Scouting units in public housing projects was begun, and special efforts were made to recruit in black communities and

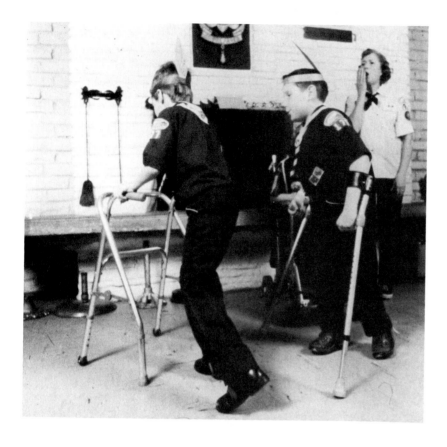

among Puerto Ricans, Mexican-Americans, and Cuban refugees. Many local councils hired professionals whose chief duty was to organize in the inner city, especially among blacks and Hispanics. At the same time, the Inner-City Rural Program was aiming at poor youth in Appalachia, the Ozarks, and other poverty pockets in rural areas.

The inner-city effort had precedents in some local councils. From 1939 to 1940, for example, the Buffalo, N.Y., Council used a bequest to rent a former convent and establish the Larkin Scout House, which became the headquarters for 13 new troops in Buffalo's core area. Albion Ende, who was in charge of the Scout House, remembered, "Most of the kids were really poor. But generally speaking they were excellent kids, and disciplinary problems were few and far between."

By the late 1960's, poverty was not the only problem in the inner cities. In some major cities, youth gangs ruled whole neighborhoods and they were hostile to symbols of the establishment like Scouting. Boy Scouts in uniform became targets for taunts and sometimes physical attacks; the tenth point of the Scout Law, "A Scout is brave," took on new meaning for them.

Still, where adult leaders could be found, Scouting thrived even in this inhospitable environment. In Chicago, for example, Clarence Phillips single-handedly managed two packs, two troops, and an Explorer post in an all-black housing project. To do it, he had to ignore gang warnings against

With a Boy Scout looking on, a Webelos Scout practices artificial respiration on a training dummy.

trying to recruit their members, the smashing of his car windows, and slashing of his tires.

"I'm going to turn all these gang boys into Boy Scouts," Phillips vowed. "After all, a Scout troop is nothing but a gang—a gang under proper supervision . . . a gang with direction." He didn't manage to turn all the gangs into Scouts but he did enroll 25 percent of the boys in the housing project, including former members of the Cobras and Junior Vice Lords.

In north-central Philadelphia, 30 gangs terrorized residents of their turfs or neighborhoods and, incidentally, decimated the ranks of church-sponsored packs and troops because no Scout dared venture onto gang turf. So the local council turned to "block Scouting," organizing Cub Scout dens and Boy Scout patrols in a single block. The dens and patrols met on the streets and porches within their own block.

In New York City's South Bronx, packs and troops were meeting in a store-front headquarters within a couple of blocks of the nation's meanest streets. In some cities, roving professionals in vans called Scoutmobiles brought the program to poor neighborhoods and housing projects. Explorer posts were organized for the young men in training programs of the Job Corps, one of the spinoffs from President Lyndon B. Johnson's War on Poverty.

The Boy Scouts of America was striving, with much success, to shed its image as an organization primarily for middle-class whites. A large percentage of the urban poor were blacks, and during the fifties and sixties tens of thousands of black boys were drawn into Scouting. In 1961 the BSA's Inter-Racial Service, which had spearheaded early efforts to enroll blacks in Scouting, metamorphosed into the Urban Relationships Service. Its scope was also broadened to include all youth in the inner city—blacks, whites, and Hispanics.

Scouting was also reaching outside its own membership to help poor boys. Beginning in 1966, many local councils opened their camps to non-Scouts and increased their subsidies for needy Scouts; 3 years later 41,000 nonmembers and poor Scouts were enjoying summer camp.

Another disadvantaged group—the handicapped—was receiving more attention, too. Physically handicapped boys had been members from Scouting's earliest years. There was a troop in the Kentucky School for the Blind in 1911 and others were established soon after in institutions for the handicapped. But no special allowances were made for handicapped Scouts until 1923 when achievement badges were created for boys with handicaps that prevented them from completing the tests for Second and First Class rank; they could not, however, earn Star, Life, or Eagle badges.

Disabilities did not keep some boys from becoming excellent Boy Scouts. Otis H. Chidester, who was a teacher and dormitory supervisor at the Arizona School for the Deaf and Blind during the late thirties, said that he led a very active, 65-member Boy Scout troop, a Sea Scout ship, and a Cub pack at the Tucson school. "When there was a district camporee for Boy Scouts," he remembered, "the deaf boys won first place and the blind boys second place for 4 years in a row for proficiency in Scouting."

In 1951, handicapped boys got a new incentive when further modifications were made in the Boy Scout advancement program. Local councils were permitted to approve them for advancement to Second and First Class, even if they couldn't fully meet the requirements. By this time, handicapped units were flourishing in institutions and thousands of moderately handicapped boys were members of ordinary troops.

The Reverend Leslie G. Shearer, of Oklahoma, makes Scouting a central part of his ministry. "I'm not going to push boys into the church," he says, "but I'm going to open the door."

Explorer Richard Chappelle points to Antarctica, where he was official Scout participant in the International Geophysical Year explorations of 1957 and 1958.

Fifteen years later the rules for a handicapped boy's advancement were further eased. A boy whose disability prevented him from passing the Swimming and Lifesaving merit badges was permitted to substitute others of equal difficulty and thus qualify for Boy Scouting's highest award, the Eagle Scout badge. (This rule was later rescinded, only to be reinstated in 1979.) In 1970 the Boy Scouts of America began a concerted effort to serve more handicapped boys when a full-time professional was added to the national staff with a grant from the Disabled American Veterans.

The BSA marked its 60th anniversary that year. There were nearly 6.3 million members for the celebration, but the first blip had appeared on the membership charts the previous year. Enrollment dropped slightly in 1969, the first loss in 59 years; it was recovered with lots to spare in the next 3 years.

The baby boom's effects were spent, though, and boys were no longer gravitating naturally toward Scouting as a rite of passage into adulthood. Little League baseball and other junior sports programs were beginning to affect the rate at which boys joined Scouting and their tenure in its programs. The halcyon days were over for the Boy Scouts of America, as they were for the other mainline organizations in American life.

Off to Camps of
High Adventure

Campers pause by a roaring river near Bissett base in Canada.

Canoeing and Camping in the North Country

Surrounded by vast areas of unspoiled lakes and rivers near Lake Superior, two canoeing camps—Charles L. Sommers National High Adventure Base, 6 miles from the Minnesota-Canada border, and Boulder Junction, in northern Wisconsin—offer wilderness instruction and excitement to boys and girls 13 and over. More than 20,000 Scouts each year challenge themselves here and at the BSA's other "High Adventure" bases in Maine, New Mexico, and Florida.

Above, Scouts are instructed in basic canoe skills before heading out on a trip.

Below, two paddlers muscle down a Canadian lake with a passenger and a heavy pack.

Leaping off a lakeside cliff, a camper forsakes form for sheer fun.

Above, a successful fisherman
shows what he caught for dinner—two pike. Right: campers
angle from a canoe.

Wild blueberries picked in the Canadian wilds.

Living Off the Land and the Water

Three- to seven-day canoe excursions among pristine Wisconsin lakes and campsites are the easiest fare offered by the North Country camps. Most trips last a week to 10 days, and for Scouts and Explorers 16 and over, Sommers camp offers a special 21-day Nor'wester Program. It involves backpacking in the Porcupine Mountains of Michigan's Upper Peninsula or hiking on Isle Royale in Lake Superior, followed by a canoe trek through northern Minnesota and training in rock-climbing at the Sommers base. For the truly dauntless, Sommers also has a winter camping program. No matter how rugged the journey or experienced the campers, though, all crews are instructed and assisted by specially trained guides and counselors—and all participants can depend on eating the finest fresh food during their outings, as the photographs here show. The Boy Scouts' camping experience in the area goes back to 1923—a canoe trip that summer in northern Minnesota grew into an annual event that eventually led to the founding of the Sommers base in 1942.

At the end of the day, the blueberries gathered are made into a sweet stew.

181

Two Scouts in a flexible canoe (opposite), equipped with helmets and flotation jackets, race into white water on a Maine river. The canoe swamps and turns over, near left, after veering across the river, but the Scouts, well prepared, are in little danger. One of them, right, immediately begins the search for his lost paddle.

Chilly Thrills in Maine

Maine's High Adventure program is for crews that want little coddling—there are no "standard" trips, and each group, though accompanied by a High Adventure guide, is expected to supply its own expedition leader. Travel depends on strength of arms and legs and fitness of body. Two bases, Matagamon, near Baxter State Park, and Seboomook, to the west, push campers off into exploration of the state's rugged, sparsely settled interior, with its mountains and lakes and its moose, deer, bear, and eagles; trips from the St. Croix base, near the coast, include travel and fishing along waterways shared with Canada. Most trips are scheduled for June, July, or August, but, as at Sommers, winter expeditions may also be arranged. Maine extends a special challenge to youngsters 13 through 17 with a yen for white water and a tolerance for blackflies, and in the cold months, there's the excitement of cross-country skiing, building snow shelters, and camping out in the snow.

Striking camp, Scouts prepare for another day of travel. The tents are all provided by the BSA at the base, as are canoes, packs, paddles, food, maps, and most other equipment.

After shinnying up a palm tree (left), a Scout shakes a coconut—if there's a sloshing sound, the fruit inside is ready to be picked and eaten.

Freshly trapped lobsters form the heart of an evening meal.

Cruising on a 44-foot ketch, Scouts make the boat their home for 7 days, learning navigation, ship handling, and how to troll for fish.

Sailing in the Florida Sun

Located on Lower Matecumbe Key, some 75 miles south of Miami, the Florida Sea Base introduces Scouts to the aquatic world of the subtropics. Just a mile from the base, a living, underwater coral garden forms a protective barrier reef, one of the world's most complex and beautiful environments. A variety of shallow and deep-water diving expeditions head there and elsewhere—all with licensed captains and qualified instructors. The base has its own fleet of large and small craft, and campers can sail off on a cruise, take a course in boat handling, or head north to the Everglades in canoes. The Mariner Sailing Adventure is particularly popular. It gives a crew of up to nine youngsters the chance to learn to sail their own 25-foot boat around the keys. New in 1984 is the Out Island Adventure, which combines a sailing program at the Sea Base with a primitive campout of 4 days on a wild island beyond the horizon.

The day's sailing done, a young chef prepares a feast.

Riders embark on a Cavalcade, an 8-day journey made entirely on horseback.

Philmont's High-Country Challenge

In 1938 and 1942, an Oklahoma oilman named Waite Phillips gave the BSA over 125,000 acres of land in the mountains and mesas of New Mexico, "for the purpose of perpetuating faith, self-reliance, integrity, freedom, principles used to build this great country by the American Pioneer." The land became Philmont Scout Ranch, to which more than 500,000 Scouts have since gone for backpacking, rock climbing, gold panning, and other rugged activities.

The 12,441-foot summit of "the Tooth of Time", Philmont's highest peak, rises behind two backpackers.

Hikers pass through a flowery meadow among the mountains of Philmont.

As his companions look on, a Scout prepares to rappel down from the top of a cliff.

Heading for the Hills

Philmont's Expeditions, 12-day backpacking trips, cover some of the most rugged of the ranch's 300 miles of high-altitude trails. Along the way, campers can climb mountains 2 miles high, scale rock cliffs, pan for gold in icy streams, ride horses western style, excavate for Indian artifacts, fish for mountain trout—and catch their breath at stunning New Mexico sunrises and sunsets. The trips are graded by difficulty—typical, rugged, strenuous, and super strenuous—and are open to any Scout or Explorer 13 or over in good physical condition.

Partway down, the rappeller adjusts his rope.

Hikers toss their shoes on high at the end of an expedition.

Alone with the immensity of nature, two hikers watch the sun go down near Philmont Ranch.

7

Scouting in the Space Age

From the experience gained in our Inner-City Rural projects and other research, all of us realized the challenge. . . . We would have to be bold, imaginative, resourceful, flexible, reasonable, and above all—realistic. Furthermore, we must not lose our "cool" or "get uptight" over imagined threats to our traditional methods and the symbols of our movement as long as there was not a clear danger to our basic aims.
— Chief Scout Executive Alden G. Barber, 1971

ON THE NIGHT of July 20, 1969, the 35,000 Boy Scouts, Explorers, and leaders encamped at Farragut State Park in Idaho for the seventh national jamboree were supposed to be at jamboree troop campfires celebrating world friendship. A lot of them had a different interest. Like Americans everywhere, they were glued to television sets. At scattered sites around the huge tent city, the blue flicker of portable TV's drew clusters of boys and men into the charged atmosphere of an impending historic event.

All eyes were on the Apollo 11 spaceship parked on the moon. A cheer went up as astronaut Neil A. Armstrong, an Eagle Scout, clambered out of the ship in his bulky spacesuit and became the first man to set foot on the moon. He was soon followed on the moon's surface by Edwin E. (Buzz) Aldrin, Jr., another former Boy Scout. Earlier that day, Armstrong and Aldrin had radioed greetings to the jamboree Scouts and Scouters.

An aviation Scout in a glider banks into a curve above Texas.

The hot-air balloon of Explorer Post 378, in Albuquerque, soars over New Mexico.

The contrast between the advanced technology represented by the moon walkers and the Scoutcraft being practiced by the latter-day disciples of Baden-Powell, Seton, and Beard 241,000 miles away symbolized a question facing the Boy Scouts of America: Was Scouting in tune with the times?

Not that Scouting lagged far behind in scientific interests; in 1969, a Boy Scout could earn merit badges in Atomic Energy, Computers, and Space Exploration. Rather, the question was whether Scouting's programs were attuned to the needs and desires of youth in the space age. "Relevance" was the buzz word of the times, not only in Scouting but in churches, universities, and other bulwarks of American society.

A study for the BSA's national Executive Board by the research firm of Daniel Yankelovich, Inc., found that while Scouting was highly regarded by an overwhelming majority of Americans, both young and old, there were signs that all was not well. Researchers found a high dropout rate and were told by boys that "Scouting teaches a lot of things you never get to use afterward" . . . "Scouting gets boring" . . . "Scouting is too organized" . . . "Scouting is a lot of fun at first but after a while it isn't fun anymore" . . . "Scouting is kind of out of date."

Furthermore, the study reported, many boys and young men believed that Scouting's programs pointed not toward adulthood but backward toward childhood. The older the boy, the less likely he was to find Scouting's programs compatible with his interests and view of the future.

These findings reflected changes in American society and particularly in the attitudes of youth. When Neil Armstrong walked on the moon, colleges were in turmoil, with student strikes, demands for more power for the young, and marches and draft-card burnings in protest of America's involvement in the Vietnam War. There was much talk of a "generation gap" separating the young from their elders in matters of values, morals, and attitudes toward work. While the unrest was centered on college campuses, its effects spilled over into the high schools and even to junior-high-age children.

The continuing civil rights revolution and its offshoots—the women's movement and demands for equal rights and access to power by Hispanics, American Indians, homosexuals, the handicapped, and other minority populations—raised challenges to cherished beliefs and attitudes during the 1970's. The national trauma of Watergate further undermined the old values. Family life was changing as single-parent families and households with both husband and wife employed outside the home became common.

The Yankelovich study and the BSA's continuing efforts to reach more boys in the nation's ghettos and poor rural areas demonstrated the movement's striving for relevance in the 1970's. They also brought about significant changes in Scouting's priorities and concerns.

Some were minor. In Cub Scouting, for example, the pledge "to be square" was dropped from the Cub Scout Promise because "square" had become a pejorative, suggesting someone hopelessly out of it in the post-hippie era. The word "boy" was eased out of "Boy Scout" and "Scouting/USA" was adopted in 1976 as the movement's label for most communications purposes. Scouting/USA was thought to be more descriptive than

"Boy Scouts of America" for an organization that included girls in the Exploring program and women in many leadership positions. For corporate purposes, "Boy Scouts of America" remained in use.

In its quest for relevance, the Boy Scouts of America tackled the drug abuse epidemic among the young, launching a program called "Operation Reach" in the spring of 1972. Its purpose was to show how the superficial highs of drugs could be replaced by warm and open relationships with parents, strong friendships, and a sense of belonging to something bigger than oneself, such as Scouting.

Most Cub Scout packs, Scout troops, and Explorer posts formed in the nation's inner cities during the early 1970's were indistinguishable from those in small towns and suburbs. But a few had their own agendas based on ethnic pride. Troop 503 in Brooklyn, N.Y., recited both the standard Scout Oath and its own troop pledge: "On my honor, I will do my best to help my brother and sister at all times, and to help build up my community and my nation." Dubbing themselves the Black and Puerto Rican Stoners (because they intended to be as hard and solid as stone), the Scouts of Troop 503 wore Army-style fatigues, combat boots, and green berets. Thus were local troops, in small but significant ways, doing old things differently. In Milwaukee, an all-black "Super Troop" learned judo, karate, and Afro-American history and camped in the inner city rather than in the woods. They, too, devised a distinctive uniform with black berets, gold shoulder braid, and combat boots. A regular Good Turn for Detroit's Martin Luther King Explorer Post was escorting elderly welfare recipients as they picked up their checks.

The most profound effect of the Yankelovich study and the search for relevance, however, was a sweeping overhaul of the Boy Scout program in 1972. The overhaul was aimed at making Boy Scouting flexible enough to meet the needs and desires of boys everywhere—in the inner city, suburb, and rural regions, among rich and poor, black and white.

Scout activities for Mississippi Choctaws include learning tribal dances, as shown here. Indian leaders say Scouting helps both to sustain traditions and teach modern skills.

There were several elements: a drastic revision of the advancement plan for Boy Scouts; greater emphasis on decision-making by the boys; less stress on outdoor skills and more on home and community; and provision of a "leadership corps" for older boys in the troop.

A new Boy Scout manual, the eighth edition since 1911, was published under the title *Scout Handbook*. Gone from its pages were tracking and stalking in the woods, signaling by semaphore and Morse code, canoeing and rowing, rope lashing and pioneering projects, edible plants, tree identification, and first aid for sunstroke, heat exhaustion, and frostbite. The handbook replaced those traditional skills with advice on drug abuse and first aid for rat bites, and how to take a hike in the city, tackle community problems, introduce a guest speaker at a troop meeting, and assist parents in everyday family life.

From the Boy Scout's standpoint, the most significant changes were in the advancement plan. No longer did he have to follow a rigid path to First Class rank (now called progress award). Under the new plan, he had choices to make all along the way from Tenderfoot to Eagle. Heretofore, merit badges had been reserved for Second Class and above; now the Tenderfoot Scout was eligible to earn merit badges.

The subject matter for advancement in the lower ranks was broken into 12 fields called skill awards, and for each one he earned, the boy received recognition in the form of a belt loop. Skill award subjects included Citizenship, Family Living, Community Living, Communications, and Environment as well as the traditional fields of First Aid, Hiking, Camping, Cooking, Conservation, Physical Fitness, and Swimming. The skill awards encompassed most of the old Scoutcraft skills, but because the boy could choose the ones he wanted to work on, it was possible to become a First Class Scout without ever going hiking or camping or cooking over an open fire. (But that probably didn't happen very often because a boy would be unlikely to remain in a troop long enough to reach First Class if he never hiked or camped.)

The revised program had important implications for Scout leaders, too. The Scoutmaster's role was to be more that of counselor and guide than expert in Scoutcraft and all things outdoors. As one veteran Scoutmaster put it, "We're going to have to bring into Scouting men who will probably be very good at this counseling phase of it, but men who probably couldn't cook a piece of bacon—and never will be able to. Too darned fastidious to like to go camping anyway."

The heart of the leader's counseling job was in the "personal growth agreement conference" as the final step in a Scout's advancement to the next progress award. The Scoutmaster's task was to help the Boy Scout assess his own strengths and weaknesses and set new goals for himself, both in Scouting and in everyday life. The personal growth agreement conference was not entirely new, but previously the Scoutmaster had not been expected to be concerned so much with the boy's future outside of Scouting.

The new leadership corps bore a striking resemblance to the Senior Scouts and Explorer patrols in troops of the thirties and forties. The leadership corps was open to boys 14 and 15 years old who would serve as

Scouts from Puerto Rico (above) make a splint as described in the 1979 Boy Scout Handbook, *written by William "Green Bar Bill" Hillcourt (below).*

The new Handbook *emphasizes the outdoor activities that have always been at the heart of Scouting. At left is a "monkey bridge" made according to the book.*

instructors for the younger Scouts, do community service, and have special activities such as rugged backpacking trips, canoe expeditions, and social events.

Advanced training courses for Scoutmasters, and later for the young troop and patrol leaders, were revised to include lessons in 11 leadership competencies, or skills—counseling, communicating, planning, evaluating, and the like. Leaders were encouraged to see themselves as "managers of learning" rather than primarily as outdoorsmen.

The changes in Boy Scouting got mixed reviews from leaders. Some, like Roundtable Commissioner Neil W. Erickson of Manitowoc, Wis., saw great value in the skill award idea because it gave the Scout immediate recognition for passing a test en route to his next progress award. "Scouts are advancing at a rate comparable to, or faster than, advancement in the old program," he wrote to *Scouting* magazine. "The short-term goals of the skill award system keep interest and competitive spirit very much alive." Other leaders were enthusiastic over the revised program's potential for boys in the inner city.

But some were outraged. "I am appalled," wrote Scoutmaster Carl A. Schroeder of Buffalo, N.Y., "at the changes that have been made under the guise of 'upgrading' the advancement program. A Scout may now wear First Class insignia without a knowledge of the knife and ax, without ever taking a hike, lighting a fire, cooking an outdoor meal, or ever sleeping under canvas. But worst of all, the Eagle rank, respected throughout the country as a top-notch achievement for youth, has been cheapened drastically. By the elimination of Camping, Cooking, Nature and other [merit] badges heretofore required, a Scout may become an Eagle virtually without ever setting foot past his city line."

SCOUTING WAS NEVER IN TUNE WITH THE TIMES

In 1969 we came out with research with the title, "Is Scouting in Tune With the Times?" Scouting had never been in tune with the times! Even in 1908 it was idiotic to suggest that you should go out and do camping because everybody knew that the night air was bad for you—you might get malaria, for heaven's sake. The only ones who did camping were these idiots who wanted to explore the world and the military who *had* to go camping. The idea of cooking your meal over an open fire when your mother at home was perfectly willing to cook your meal over a coal fire, and this idea of sitting around a campfire when you had a perfectly good kerosene lamp burning in your living room at home—it was exactly because it was idiotic and out of tune with the times that made Scouting appealing. It goes back to the atavistic thing that is supposed to be in every human being to play Tarzan and Robinson Crusoe and so on.

—William (Green Bar Bill) Hillcourt,
Retired National Director of Scoutcraft,
Manlius, N.Y.

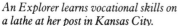
An Explorer learns vocational skills on a lathe at her post in Kansas City.

Such strong feelings were widespread among veteran Scoutmasters and brought a cautionary note from Mark H. Rowland, a commissioner in Cedar Rapids, Iowa: "I must comment that even those who do not share my opinion of the immense good to be derived from the program improvements might consider that the continued expression of resentment, bitterness and the 'It always worked such and such a way for us' syndrome will neither continue to improve the program nor strengthen existing qualities. . . ."

The Scouting program revisions did not affect the week-to-week operation of strong troops in significant ways. "The changes did cause us some problems, but I couldn't put my finger on it," recalled William J. Tucker, who was then Scoutmaster of Troop 26 chartered to Elliott Avenue Baptist Church in Springfield, Ill. "We continued to teach and learn the outdoor skills, and we went camping every month, just as we always had," he explained. "We did feel that the new *Scout Handbook* was diluted and did not have as many things in it as the old ones had. But I don't think our troop lost anything because of it."

Nor did every inner-city troop take to the program changes. Some, like Houston's all-black Troop 242, continued with the old program of regular hikes, campouts, and concentration on advancement that produced six or seven Eagle Scouts each year, far above the national average.

In the view of an experienced professional Scouter, the revised Boy Scout program was excellent for boys who were good students and who were led by young executives with talents for management. "But," he added, "the average Scout leader suffered. He didn't know how to become a manager of learning, a consultant. The average Scoutmaster emphasized camping skills. He did not view the new program as beneficial when his troop was primarily interested in how to survive a week or weekend in the woods no matter what the weather."

Hundreds of disaffected Scoutmasters dropped out, and the number of Boy Scouts declined precipitously in the years following the introduction of the revised program. Traditionalists pointed to the program changes, arguing that they had taken the romance out of Scouting. But other factors were at work since enrollment in Cub Scouting was declining, too.

The most influential of the revised program's opponents was William Hillcourt, retired national director of Scoutcraft and the movement's best-known figure. A native of Denmark who had joined the national staff in 1926 and, as "Green Bar Bill," had been a fixture in the pages of *Boys' Life* for 5 decades, William Hillcourt was a highly visible and outspoken champion of Scouting's traditional program. He was author of 12 books on Scouting, including the *Boy Scout Handbook* edition displaced by the new *Scout Handbook*, as well as earlier editions of the *Scoutmaster's Handbook*, *Handbook for Patrol Leaders*, and the *Scout Fieldbook*.

His urgings, and protests by many Scouters, both volunteer and professional, that the Boy Scout program had strayed too far from its origins, brought a reversal of course under the leadership of Chief Scout Executive Harvey L. Price. (Price had succeeded Alden G. Barber in 1976; Barber had been CSE since the retirement of Joseph A. Brunton, Jr., in 1969.) In 1978, advancement requirements were changed again to make outdoor skills mandatory; Scouts would have to earn the Hiking, First Aid, Camping and Cooking skill awards to make First Class.

The following year, the *Scout Handbook* was scrapped. It was replaced by *The Official Boy Scout Handbook*, written by William Hillcourt, with advice from a task force of volunteers and professionals. Hillcourt contributed a year of his time and his formidable enthusiasm for the old ways of Scouting. Back in the basic Scout manual were signaling, mapmaking, tracking and stalking, and other skills practiced by Boy Scouts since 1910, although they were not required for advancement to First Class. Most of the skills oriented toward city life were retained, but the new handbook was redolent of Boy Scouting's old emphasis on camping and life in woods and fields.

Troop leaders continued to learn the 11 skills of leadership in their advanced training, but the idea that they should be primarily "managers of learning" was abandoned. Once again they were expected to be outdoorsmen, although with some knowledge of how to counsel, plan, and evaluate.

The back-to-basics trend exemplified by *The Official Boy Scout Handbook* received a generally enthusiastic reception, even from leaders who had seen considerable value in the effort to make Scouting more flexible and relevant to inner-city boys.

A police officer shows two Memphis Explorers how to take fingerprints.

At top, a New Jersey Scout collects steel cans to aid the BSA's 1970s nationwide conservation drive, Project SOAR (Saving Our American Resources); above, a Scout at a camporee saves energy an old-fashioned way.

The Yankelovich study had indicated that no major surgery was needed for Cub Scouting; in general, the program was found to be in line with the interests of boys 8 to 10 years old. Beginning in 1973, more outdoor activity away from the home was suggested for Cub Scouts, and Cub Scout day camps began appearing in local councils. Later, some councils established resident summer camps for Cub Scouts, a move that had been frowned upon in Cubbing's early days.

In another departure from tradition, Cub Scouting leadership positions were opened to women. In 1973, women were authorized to serve as liaison between pack and sponsor and as Cub Scouting commissioners. Three years later women Cubmasters were approved.

Throughout the seventies, the basics of Cub Scouting were unchanged, although a simplified *Wolf Cub Scout Book* for 8-year-olds was introduced in 1978. Then in 1982, two major changes were made. One involved a great expansion of the advancement possibilities for 9-year-olds, giving them 12 additional achievements to work on for the Bear rank. The other change was the introduction of an entirely new program for 7-year-old boys called Tiger Cubs BSA.

The Tiger Cubs program called for the boy and an adult member of his family to join with others in his group for a monthly field trip or other special event. Programs were centered on 17 "big ideas" with such titles as "Know Your Community," "Fitness and Sports," "Family Entertainment," and "Prepare for Emergencies." All activities were informal events planned by the parents. The only uniform part worn was a T-shirt with a Tiger Cubs decal on it.

Each Tiger Cubs group was loosely affiliated with a Cub Scout pack, but joint meetings were held only twice a year—once for the pack's Blue and Gold dinner marking Scouting's anniversary in February and again in late spring when the Tiger Cubs were eligible to join the pack.

Tiger Cubs BSA grew rapidly from the start; within 4 months 84,000 boys and parents joined, and during the first 2 full years more than 200,000 were enrolled.

Exploring, which had evolved out of Boy Scouting during the long search for an answer to the "older boy problem," found its metier with the introduction of career-interest Exploring in 1959 and the addition of girls 10 years later. In the process, Exploring gradually shifted direction.

What had begun as advanced Scouting for young men, with liberal dollops of community service, career exploration, and social events, was increasingly a coed program focused on careers. By the early 1970's, more than 100,000 girls were Explorers and nearly half of all posts centered their activities on a career or avocation.

This trend has continued to the present day. Roughly half of Exploring's membership today is female (a few posts are all-girl), and the vast majority of posts are career-oriented. Even among the "traditional" posts that feature outdoor skills, many have specialties—backpacking, rock climbing, or canoeing.

Because so few traditional posts were left, a new program called Varsity Scouting was introduced in 1984 for boys 14 through 17 years old who wanted to continue in Boy Scouting but with more advanced activities than younger Scouts could handle. Despite its title, Varsity Scouting had no sports associations other than nomenclature; Varsity Scouts were organized into squads and teams, and the leaders were a man called Coach instead of Scoutmaster, and a boy called team captain instead of senior patrol leader. Varsity Scouts continued on the Boy Scout advancement trail toward Eagle and enjoyed backpacking and canoeing treks and other outdoor pursuits beyond the capabilities of younger Boy Scouts. In many ways, the new program harked back to the Exploring of the 1950's.

During the seventies, while enrollment in Boy Scouting and Cub Scouting was dropping sharply, Exploring's membership fluctuated in the 400,000 to 500,000 range. But the career focus was catching on, and scores of large corporations as well as local companies saw the value of introducing young people to the adult world of work. Such giants of industry as General Motors, IBM, Western Electric, McDonnell Douglas, U.S. Steel, United Airlines, and Sears, Roebuck sponsored posts for various career interests in many of their local branches.

Thousands of career-interest posts were organized in such diverse fields as accounting, engineering, computers, business, science, auto mechanics, electronics, communications, banking, secretarial work, photography, and journalism under sponsorship of business and industry. Hospitals and medical societies backed posts for medical and health career exploration. Hundreds of police agencies sponsored law enforcement posts. The airline and aircraft industries and their unions started aviation-related career posts. (Air Exploring had been phased out as a separate program in 1965.)

Still other specialty posts were formed in hobby, craft, and sports fields for young men and women interested in ham radio, music, the theater, sculpture, skiing, archery, basketball, and bowling.

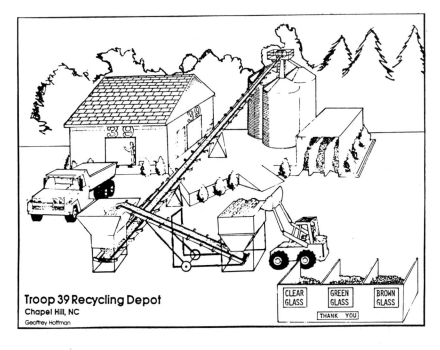

Troop 39 Recycling Depot
Chapel Hill, NC
Geoffrey Hoffman

A North Carolina Scout troop designed this glass-disposal unit for a community recycling effort and processed 1,800 tons of glass in 8 years.

201

For most of the career posts, the sponsor provided not only expert leadership but hands-on experience in its place of business. A drafting post, for example, would meet in the professional drafting room of its sponsor and use its facilities and equipment. Similarly, a medical post's meeting place would be a hospital or other health-care facility where the Explorers could watch and assist in some phases of the work.

By their very nature, many career-interest posts had a fluid membership. Young men and women joined to explore a career, and if they didn't like what they found, they moved on to another post with a different specialty. A career-interest post might maintain its enrollment total throughout the school year but end the year with fewer than half of the original members.

Exploring's scope was further expanded during the late 1970's when the program began penetrating the nation's high schools. The vehicle was career-awareness Exploring, a series of career seminars and tours during the school day. Under the aegis of the local Scout council's Exploring leaders, men and women representing various careers came into the high schools to discuss the duties, requirements, and advantages of their professions or trades. Students who were interested in exploring a field in more depth were urged to join a post specializing in that career.

At the same time, in cooperation with the U.S. Office of Education, Exploring offered in-school career education in high schools. In this program, Explorer posts were organized for classes, homerooms, or career clubs, but otherwise the program was the same as career-awareness Exploring in its design, aiming to expose the students to a variety of careers through classroom presentations and field trips to local businesses and industries.

With the impetus provided by its programs in high schools and the growing concern of young people about their future, Exploring enjoyed phenomenal membership growth during the early 1980's. Annual gains were in the 25 to 30 percent range, and it was predicted that enrollment in Exploring would pass Boy Scouting's during the nineties.

The Boy Scouts of America also made progress during the seventies and early eighties in serving handicapped youth. More than 60,000 handicapped persons were enrolled in packs, troops, and posts sponsored by institutions and community organizations, and an estimated 150,000 others were members of mainstream units.

Booklets were produced to guide leaders in their work with the mentally retarded, the deaf, the blind, and those with other physical handicaps. In 1974 the National Advisory Committee on Scouting for the Handicapped (NACOSH) was formed with representatives from leading national organizations and governmental agencies for the disabled.

Some Scout troops and Explorer posts "adopted" Scouting units for the handicapped in institutions. Among units with the longest tradition of aiding the handicapped is Troop 162, chartered to Good Shepherd Lutheran Church of Tulsa, Okla. Troop 162 has held an annual camporee for mentally retarded "Special Scouts" from eight Oklahoma institutions since 1969.

Age restrictions were removed for all severely handicapped persons in 1978 so that they could continue in Scouting's programs beyond the normal cutoff ages of 11 for Cub Scouts, 18 for Boy Scouts, and 21 for

Cub Scouts from East Windsor, N. J., above, compete in a space derby, racing their homemade, gravity-powered spaceships down tracks of string. At right, one of the Cubs puts finishing touches on his craft. As in a pinewood derby, the experience teaches Cubs not only woodworking but also aerodynamics.

Explorers. (Age limits for the mentally retarded had been lifted in 1965, and 50-year-old Cub Scouts were common in institutions.) The end of the age limit for all severely disabled persons followed the widely publicized case of a 23-year-old cerebral palsy victim in Roosevelt, N.Y., who had been denied an Eagle Scout badge after earning 24 merit badges because he was overage. A year later, the BSA's national Executive Board approved substitution of required merit badges for disabled Boy Scouts seeking the Eagle Scout award, making it possible for many physically handicapped boys to earn Scouting's top prize.

Efforts were also made to give Scouting's ablebodied members an understanding of the problems faced by handicapped persons. At national jamborees and local council camporees, ablebodied Scouts and Explorers were invited to travel "handicapped awareness trails" wearing blindfolds, having an arm immobilized, steering a wheelchair, or being otherwise temporarily handicapped. In 1981 a Handicapped Awareness merit badge was

In 1982, the BSA began admitting 7-year-olds as Tiger Cubs. Here, one poses with the animal version.

made available for Scouts who sought to learn how to deal with disabled persons in a positive way.

The traditions of doing national Good Turns and holding a national jamboree every 4 years continued through the turbulent seventies and into the eighties. But they, too, were affected by the mandate to bring Scouting in tune with the times.

The major Good Turn of the 1970's was Project SOAR (Save Our American Resources), a conservation campaign. Unlike previous national Good Turns, it was not limited to a span of a few weeks or months; the SOAR campaign was renewed each year. Also unlike earlier national conservation projects going back to the early days of Scouting in America, SOAR was not limited to tree planting, erosion control, and habitat improvement on open lands.

Words like "ecology," "ecosystem," and "biosphere" were appearing in Boy Scout literature as the environmental movement made Americans aware of the problems of pollution of air, water, and land and the limits of natural resources. In Project SOAR, the BSA addressed these problems. Tens of thousands of packs, troops, and posts in both city and suburb cleaned up littered streams and the borders of highways, planted trees and shrubs to slow erosion, and restored millions of acres of urban parks to their natural beauty.

Especially popular were collections of scrap materials for recycling. Thousands of units established regular collections of wastepaper, aluminum, or glass for recycling. Such collections became even more important following the Arab oil embargo of 1973 when Project SOAR's emphasis turned to energy conservation because much less energy is required for recycling most products than for refining raw materials.

Today an estimated one-fourth of all Scout troops have periodic recycling collections. Sometimes their motives go beyond energy conservation.

Troop 1 of North Caldwell, N.J., which, come hail, high water, or holiday, has collected wastepaper, glass, and aluminum on the first Saturday of every month since 1973, earns 75 percent of the troop budget from scrap. But, said Scoutmaster Tom Potenzone of Troop 1, which is chartered to the North Caldwell Board of Education, "our main purpose is to keep recyclable trash from going to the dumps. The dumps in New Jersey are becoming full. If we take 15 tons of scrap away from the dumps every month, maybe we'll get another year out of our landfills before they're closed and the trash has to be taken farther away at a bigger cost to homeowners."

National statistics were not kept for Project SOAR participation, but more than 60,000 packs, troops, and posts were estimated to have undertaken a conservation project each year.

Scoutcraft competitions and huge arena shows featuring stars like Bob Hope and Burl Ives were the highlights of the national jamborees of 1973, 1977, and 1981. But these old favorites were joined by such innovations as competitions for arts, crafts, and sciences, cooking contests using chemical stoves, boiling water with solar heat, and measuring by the metric system. Perhaps the most startling innovation was electronic pathfinding; Scouts set aside their compasses and used directional radios to find hidden signal senders.

The 1973 jamboree was a doubleheader, with a total of 64,000 Scouts, Explorers, and leaders at two sites—Moraine State Park in western Pennsylvania and Farragut State Park in Idaho. The 1977 jamboree was at Moraine again and drew 28,000; in 1981 more than 30,000 were at Fort A.P. Hill, Va., for the tenth national jamboree.

The 1970's were a testing time for the Boy Scouts of America as they were for other established institutions. The BSA's membership dropped sharply, touching bottom at 4.27 million in 1979. The enrollment decline reflected changes in society as well as a 10 percent decrease in the number of Scouting-age youth. Sports programs such as Little League baseball and junior football, soccer, basketball, and other diversions forced many boys to choose between Scouting and other activities. The nation's economy was sluggish, with rampant inflation and high unemployment rates, causing a drop in contributions to voluntary organizations like the Boy Scouts of America.

But the BSA weathered the seventies with its bedrock values intact and its appeal for youth still strong. Late in the decade, a conservative trend was discernible in America. There were indications of a return to the values long espoused by the BSA—patriotism, self-discipline, respect for authority, and duty to God, community, and country. In 1982 James Shriver of the Gallup Poll's Youth Survey reported, "We've been finding broad support for traditional American values among the students we've been questioning."

With the resurgence of the old values, the BSA's membership decline was stopped and a slow but steady increase began. During the early 1980's, annual gains were in the 1 to 4 percent range, and, as the Boy Scouts of America prepared to celebrate its 75th anniversary, it had about 4.8 million members.

Kansas City, Mo., Cubs watch finalists speed by in a council-wide pinewood derby championship. The handmade cars may weigh up to 5 ounces—and not one grain more.

8
Today and Tomorrow

Not long ago a reporter asked me why I was still in Scouting, even though my son—now in his thirties—was the original reason I joined. "I'm still active," I told him, "because what Scouting is all about is character-building that helps youngsters find the values they need to grow up to be good men." Unfortunately, character and values are sometimes considered irrelevant in today's world. But not in my world, for character and values are the heart of the Scout Oath and the Scout Law. They always have been—and I pray to God—they always will be.

—Sanford N. McDonnell, President-elect, BSA, 1984

A Scout from Portland, Ore., takes part in a week-long, 160-mile ride through the Cascade Mountains.

THE BOY SCOUT CLINGS to a gigantic ladder in the treetops overlooking the Missouri River. He looks down uncertainly. Below, his buddies call, "Come on! You can make it!" Reassured, the Scout reaches for the next timber rung and resumes his 35-foot climb.

In other parts of the camp, Scouts help one another scramble over a 12-foot wall, climb a cargo net, balance on a swinging teeter-totter, figure out how to slip through a suspended auto tire without touching it, and free-fall backward from a height of 5 feet into their buddies' arms.

The scene is Camp Geiger of the Pony Express Council, St. Joseph, Mo., and the event is Project COPE, an acronym for Challenging Outdoor Physical Encounter. Twenty-four tests of strength, agility, coordination,

Scouter Oxendine, with his daughter, helps run a single-parents weekend in North Carolina.

problem-solving ability, and courage are designed to encourage boys to reach within themselves for more than they think they have and to learn to think and act with other Scouts in a climate of mutual trust.

In Oregon's Cascade Mountains, 16 Portland Scouts on horseback follow Wilfried (Ranger Bill) Bruns over 160 miles of narrow mountain trails and logging roads in a week-long trek through some of America's most spectacular scenery. It's early July, but snow still blankets the ground in shaded nooks. On the sixth day out, the quartermaster's truck, which carries the caravan's food supplies, tents, and sleeping bags, gets mired in snow and mud 8 miles from the campsite, and the riders spend a miserable night huddled against cold and rain with nothing to eat.

Later, Scout Aric Jones says, "I'm glad we city kids had the chance to experience something like that. . . . We got to test ourselves. So we missed a dinner and one breakfast. So we got a little wet and cold. Big deal! I wouldn't have missed it for the whole world."

In New York City's South Bronx, a symbol of urban devastation during the 1970's, Boy Scout Troop 95 and Cub Scout Pack 95 sustain an oasis of good Scouting in Thessalonia Baptist Church. Even during the years when the local police precinct became known as Fort Apache, Scouting was kept alive by Cub Scout Den Leader Connie Sayles and Cubmaster John H. Lee. Says Sayles, "I try to instill in the boys the belief that you have the opportunity, you have a chance—if you need a little love, a little affection, a little pushing, I'm here to help you." Scoutmaster David A. Boone adds, "I'm in Scouting because it does one thing, and I think about this often. We remove something from a boy's life; we take away despair."

The Boy Scouts of America today is a huge umbrella covering a host of opportunities for adventure, fun, education, and service that would have amazed the men who started it all three-quarters of a century ago.

In New York City's South Bronx, a Scoutmaster briefs patrol leaders in preparation for a winter campout.

ONE MAN'S VIEW

Since I started as a Scout in St. Anthony, Idaho, in 1923, there have been changes in advancement requirements, but basically, in my mind, Scouting today serves the same purposes, and we do it almost the same way as we did then. We still give Scouts a chance to develop some initiative and learn how to take care of themselves in the circumstances.

The boys haven't changed in basic ways. I think now, as I used to think when I was a Scoutmaster in the twenties and thirties, that a boy will do anything you'll let him do, even succeed. If anything, the boys are a little sharper now. They've got more on their minds and they've had to learn more history than we did in those days. I've got a lot of confidence in the youth of today.   —*Earl E. Bagley, troop committee member, Salt Lake City, Utah*

Under that umbrella is the Sea Explorer Ship *Nauset*, a 42-foot ketch that can be seen slicing through the chill waters of Cape Cod Bay every summer weekend. It's manned by Sea Explorers from Ship 72 of Orleans, Mass., and was built a generation ago by their forebears in the group. The *Nauset* has been virtually a summer home for hundreds of Cape Cod's youth, and every year the Sea Explorers take her on a 2-week cruise among Maine's coastal islands or even farther afield to eastern Canada.

Sailing the *Nauset* is a lesson in teamwork. "When they get on this boat," says Skipper Mike Allard, "they learn to live with each other and take responsibility. They have to realize that when you're offshore in 20-foot seas and 60-mile-an-hour winds, which we've had, you've got to get your sails down *now*. You have to work together."

Some 2,000 miles west, in the Gila Wilderness of the Mogollon Mountains in southwestern New Mexico, 250 Scouts and leaders from the Sunshine District of the Yucca Council work at hard labor on a conservation project called Gila SOAR. For 7 days they engage in construction, restoration, reclamation, flood control, planting, maintenance, and improvement—jobs that were planned by the U.S. Forest Service but set aside for lack of funds and manpower. Cost to the government, $1,500; value of the work, $21,000. District Ranger S. G. Palm says, "Frankly, I'm a little awed. These were meaningful, needed projects, things we wouldn't have gotten done otherwise."

Back east in New Jersey, 70 excited youngsters pulling homemade soapbox racers mill around near a starting line on a gently sloping street, waiting for the beginning of the annual Cub Scout Cubmobile Derby of the Ocean County Council. Then, in flights of three, they race their cars down the street for fun and the hope of a trophy. Some look grim and steer for dear life. Others shout, "Yahoo!" as they happily crash through traffic cones lining the lanes. Ask 9-year-old winner Jeff Bertolini how it feels to race in the derby, and he exclaims, "It's a lot of fun!"

In Jefferson City, Mo., on a Saturday evening, KLUM-FM broadcasts "Teen Scene"—3 hours of rock music, news, and interviews planned, written, and aired by the Explorers of Radio Post 86. It's the station's longest-running show. Since 1974, Post 86 has introduced scores of young people to announcing, production, and the technical aspects of radio. Many of its alumni have gone on to become professional announcers, program directors, and engineers. Of "Teen Scene," station manager George Forster says, "I want more of it. I said that the first time I heard it."

In Long Beach, Calif., young men and adults of the National Eagle Scout Association prepare for Project Love, which brings Christmas to 7,000 children in Arizona's Navajo Indian reservation. Months of work go into planning the event and assembling and wrapping gifts, most of them donated by employees of McDonnell Douglas Corporation and other businesses. Two big tractor-trailers are needed to ferry the presents 650 miles to the reservation, and Eagle Scouts join the accompanying parade of buses and cars and help with Christmas parties at the schools. Project Love has been a tradition since 1974.

"Scoutexpo," in the twin cities of Minneapolis and St. Paul, Minn., is the lineal descendant of hundreds of Scout shows and circuses going back to Scouting's early days in America, but there are differences. For one thing, this expo is held at 10 shopping centers in the metropolitan area, all on a single day. For another, there are scores of displays and demonstrations that would have baffled Scouts of the 1920's. The old standbys are in evidence—tower-building, semaphore signaling, first-aid demonstrations, and Indian dances. But instead of the march music of the early Boy Scout bands, visitors hear big-band tunes. They see a solar water heater, an exhibition of computer programming, and a working wind tunnel.

Scouts work at erosion control in their council's effort to help preserve New Mexico's Gila Wilderness.

Meanwhile in an inner-city sixth-grade classroom in Portland, Ore., Ngoc Nguyen is winning a square-knot-tying contest. One day each week, Ngoc and his classmates enjoy an in-school Scouting period, learning knots, first aid, science and nature, citizenship lore and other Scout skills. Portland's Columbia Pacific Council is one of nearly 200 offering in-school Scouting in inner cities and other areas where transient populations, lack of resources, and a dearth of parent volunteers make traditional Scouting difficult. Says a leader of the program, "It's rewarding to know that we're touching kids who normally would not be touched, who would not be in Scouting, and we're teaching them things that will help their lives later on."

At Camp Carpenter, of the Daniel Webster Council of New Hampshire, 500 Cub Scouts pull homemade chuckwagons from "Fort Boise" to "Fort Cheyenne" as part of an annual Chuckwagon Derby. At each of six stops along the way, the "horses" become Cub Scouts again and tackle tests of first aid, bird and animal lore, knots, rescue-rope throwing, and physical fitness.

At the Cape Fear Scout Reservation in North Carolina, more than a hundred parents and their sons and daughters, few of whom are in Scouting, swim, canoe, hike, and sample the other delights of Scout camping during a semiannual Single-Parent Family Weekend. The Scout council and Family Service Agency join to give single-parent families this welcome experience of fun and togetherness. A father comments, "Being a single parent, you have less time to spend with your children than you would like. No matter what you do, you have less time. A program like this provides intense, quality time. It's a wonderful idea."

Meanwhile, in Medina, N.Y., Engineering Explorer Post 712 worries about the design of a component for a new Fisher-Price toy. The problem is to find out whether plastic is cheaper than cardboard for a tray in a toy printing kit. The Explorers work out a design, a mold is made, and a plastic tray is produced. It turns out to cost more than cardboard would,

A pack mule brought along on the Gila project carries a drowsy passenger.

ONE MAN'S VIEW

I joined Scouting in Kenya in 1922. Later I met Baden-Powell there and scouted with him. Scouting then was back to the woods, and boys today still like it. I don't think they have changed basically one bit. They are different in many ways from what I was as a child but they go for what I went for as a child. I think that in places where they've tried it people are going back to the original Baden-Powell idea. The world has changed and the boys have changed with it, but you've only got to remind them of this adventure and they go right back. It still fascinates them.

—*Norman Powell, Scoutmaster of Troop 128, Middletown, N.J.*

so the post's work is in vain. "It would have been nice had it worked," says a girl Explorer, "but now I know what engineers mean when they say, 'Back to the drawing board!'" Another Explorer comments, "I had my first opportunity to find out what engineering is really like."

Down in Virginia, 500 Boy Scouts, Webelos Scouts, and leaders pitch their tents in a farm field near Culpeper for the annual fall camporee of the National Capital Area Council's Rappahannock District. Under a cloudless sky, on an Indian summer day, the Scouts compete in log rolling, pancake flipping, cake baking, campsite-gateway construction, air-rifle marksmanship, and other events. The scene is reminiscent of thousands of similar outings beginning with the Boy Scout rallies of the 1920's. Scoutmaster Larry Wilson of Fredericksburg's Troop 1407 surveys the scene: "Anytime we have the opportunity to get Scouts together in a natural environment and do things Scouts are supposed to do, it's a worthwhile experience."

The Boy Scouts of America is all these experiences and more; it is also the 400 local councils, six regional offices, and the national headquarters in Irving, Tex., where officers and staff oversee the movement and provide the guidance and support for 133,000 Cub Scout packs, Boy Scout troops, and Explorer posts and ships. (Irving is the fourth site for the national headquarters. During the BSA's early days, the office was at 500 Fifth Avenue and later 2 Park Avenue in New York City. In 1954, it was moved to North Brunswick, N.J.; 25 years later the Texas office was opened.)

As ever, each pack, troop, and post is supported by a local institution called the chartered partner, which provides a meeting place and adult leadership. Nearly half of the chartered partners are churches, temples, and other religious bodies. Others are public and parochial schools, parent-teacher groups, civic and service organizations, and businesses.

The movement's leadership remains overwhelmingly volunteer, with fewer than 4,000 professional Scouters among the 1.13 million adult leaders.

Scoutmaster Art Barrett holds up two of the many Navaho children who have received Christmas gifts gathered by Long Beach, Calif., Eagle Scouts.

214

ONE MAN'S VIEW

When I was a boy in Troop 1, Paterson, N. J., in 1933, they taught more primitive ways of survival. Today, to keep up with the demands of the younger generation, we teach the boys what they want to know, such as electronics, aviation, and radio —whatever they want to know. In those days you had to learn Morse code and knots and other things that were really more fundamental . . . but people who have grown up from that era use knots very seldom unless they happen to be in a trade where it's required. Today, I venture to say, many boys who have attained the rank of Eagle couldn't consistently tie a square knot; they know how to do it but they couldn't do it consistently. But concentration on things like electronics, aviation, and space is meeting the needs of the modern kid.

—John Oberer, Assistant Scoutmaster,
Troop 131, Wayne, N. J.

Explorers in Missouri produce their weekly radio show, Teen Scene.

They're off! Cubs in Ocean County, N. J., compete in an annual Cubmobile Derby by racing homemade, gravity-powered cars down a 135-yard incline.

Scouts perform an Indian dance during a Scoutexpo held by local councils at 10 Minneapolis area shopping centers simultaneously.

Heading the organization is the National Council and its Executive Board. Similar volunteer bodies lead the regional and local councils.

The national organization's annual budget of $24 million is funded by members' registration and local council fees, sales of Scouting supplies, investments and interest, magazine revenues, endowments, grants, and bequests. Individual councils receive substantial aid from the United Way of America, which provides 34 percent of the more than $200 million spent locally for Scouting.

Nationwide, there are 600 Scout camps totaling 550,000 acres. Most of the camps are open year round, but summer is naturally the peak season, when 60 percent of the nation's 55,000 troops attend for a week or more. Nearly all the camps have well-supervised waterfronts for swimming, canoeing, rowing, and sailing, plus areas for archery, small-bore rifle and shotgun shooting, and orienteering with map and compass. Some also offer horseback riding, rock climbing, black-powder shooting, and outpost camping, and some give training in computers. Virtually every council conducts day camps for Cub Scouts, too, and these involve a quarter of all Cubs.

First Class Scouts who are experienced campers and Explorers who were Boy Scouts are eligible for induction into the Order of the Arrow, the BSA's national honor campers' society. They are chosen for the OA by their fellows in troop or post and become members of the local council OA lodge. The Order is renowned for service to council camps.

Older Scouts and Explorers who crave more rugged outdoor adventure than can be found in council camps may join an expedition to one of five "high adventure" bases of the Boy Scouts of America. The oldest is the Philmont Scout Ranch and Explorer Base in New Mexico. The others are in Florida, Maine, Minnesota, and Wisconsin. Opportunities vary at each base but include mountain climbing, primitive camping, backpacking treks, canoe expeditions, horseback trail riding, salt-water sailing, and scuba diving.

Scouting's alumni can join two national organizations. One is for boys and men who have earned the Eagle Scout badge and are thus eligible for the National Eagle Scout Association. Founded in 1972, NESA now has nearly 75,000 members in some 250 chapters which give service to their local councils. NESA is the successor of the Knights of Dunamis, which was founded in 1925, and a number of local council associations for Eagles.

The other national organization is Alpha Phi Omega, a service fraternity for former Scouts who are in college. APO has about 10,000 members in 350 active chapters in colleges and universities around the country. Local chapters undertake service projects, especially for the elderly and youth, including those in Scouting. Alpha Phi Omega began in 1925 at Lafayette College in Easton, Pa. It received its greatest impetus during the presidency of H. Roe Bartle, a famed Scout executive in the Kansas City, Mo., Area Council, who headed the fraternity from 1931 to 1946.

Boy Scouting's back-to-basics trend that began in 1978 did not end the organization's commitment to reach minority youth and the handicapped. Today the Urban/Rural Field Service at the national office continues to pursue the growth of Scouting in poverty areas, carrying on the job begun by the Inner-City Rural Program in the late 1960's. James L. Tarr, who succeeded Harvey L. Price as Chief Scout Executive in 1979, noted that in many cities Scouting now enrolls more blacks and low-income youth than affluent whites. One notably successful minority program has been a Hispanic Outreach campaign, for the nation's rapidly growing Latino population.

And today nearly half of all local councils have advisory committees to promote Scouting among persons with disabling conditions. Scores of councils employ professionals whose chief duty is to organize and serve units for the handicapped. For the visually impaired, *Boys' Life* magazine, *The Official Boy Scout Handbook*, some merit-badge booklets, and the three

A Portland, Ore., teacher leads an in-school Scouting meeting, bringing Scout activities to a neighborhood where they weren't always easily available.

Cub Scouts push and pull their chuckwagons from "Fort Boise" to "Cheyenne" in an annual Chuckwagon Derby in New Hampshire.

basic Cub Scout books are published in Braille and large-print editions, and are available on tape cassettes.

Scouting has also looked to the needs of the "latchkey child," who is unsupervised during the day because his parents (or single parent) work outside the home. Since 1982 hundreds of thousands of 5-to-11-year-olds, both boys and girls, have used a BSA workbook called *Prepared for Today* to learn how to cope with tasks around the home and with danger on the streets.

The Boy Scouts of America remains a major presence on the national scene. Doomsayers of the 1970's who predicted its demise as an anachronism have been confounded by its resilience. Scouting commands the allegiance of 4.84 million youths and adults despite the competing demands of sports, television, video games, and other enticements that its founders couldn't have imagined in their wildest dreams.

To ensure that the movement's appeal remains strong into the future, the BSA's national leaders began in 1982 a 16-month study of all aspects of Scouting. Four thousand volunteers and professionals scrutinized the movement's strengths and weaknesses.

Their inquiry, known as "Shaping Tomorrow," grew into 55 projects in six areas of concern: strengthening the BSA's relations with its chartered partners; improving fund-raising and financial management; making volunteer unit leaders more effective; upgrading the selection process and career opportunities for professional Scouters; increasing public awareness of Scouting's benefits; and enhancing Scouting's program offerings.

The task force offered a definition of Scouting's present-day purpose: "It is the mission of the Boy Scouts of America to serve others by helping to instill values in young people, and in other ways prepare them to make ethical choices over their lifetime in achieving their full potential."

During 1984, the Boy Scouts of America at every level, from the National Council to packs, troops, and posts, prepared to mark the organization's 75th anniversary in 1985. The theme chosen for the Diamond Jubilee was "Pride in the Past . . . Footsteps to the Future," and among the national events scheduled were a Heritage Campfire Caravan and the eleventh national jamboree. The brotherhood that Scouts feel while gathered around a campfire will be symbolized when a campfire is lighted in every state capital. Ashes from those fires will be put into boxes shaped like each of the 50 states and carried in a Campfire Caravan to the jamboree. The boxes and their ashes will then be burned at a heritage campfire before the jamboree participants, symbolizing the unity of the Scouting spirit, its brotherhood and its meaning to our nation.

Local councils and thousands of units planned special activities for the Jubilee. Among scheduled events were reunions of Scouting's alumni with their old units, special courts of honor and camporees, and displays of memorabilia from the movement's early days.

As the Boy Scouts of America enters the Jubilee year, it includes 140,000 Tiger Cubs, plus adult members of their families; 1,603,000 Cub Scouts; 1,170,000 Boy Scouts, including Varsity Scouts; 800,000 Explorers; and 1,130,000 adult leaders.

Boy Scouting, the oldest of the programs, has grown closer to the original vision of Baden-Powell and Seton in the last decade, and the fact that Boy Scouting still attracts such a substantial number of boys—urban, suburban, and rural—shows that the promise of outdoor adventure still

ONE MAN'S VIEW

When I was a Scout in the twenties, we were a lot more active in Scouting, it seems to me, because I can remember going over to my patrol leader's house 2 or 3 nights a week and really being serious about it. I believe the emphasis has shifted to more community activities, that sort of thing. Now, for some of the merit badges, you have to do a project for the community—working with a handicapped person or working at a recycling center for so many weeks. You're working for the community as a whole, outside of the troop and outside of your own activities. We had very little of that, we were so tied up with the troop. When I read about some of the changes, my first impression is, oh, they're just losing the whole spirit of Scouting. Then I realize that it's just changing from a troop-centered activity to one which is spreading out and helping other people.
—*Harold Morse, member at large,*
Watchung (N. J.) Area Council

A mother aims her camera as her son aims his bow during a North Carolina single-parents weekend.

appeals to some primal urge in the adolescent male. By all indications, Boy Scouting should thrive in the 21st century as it has since 1910.

But what will Scouting be like on its centennial in 2010? The same only different, in the judgment of James L. Tarr, who guided the movement during its period of renewed vigor and membership growth in the early 1980's. "We will still be tied to our code of values and will still be offering programs that have excitement, adventure, and challenge and an opportunity for young people to develop their potential," he said. Tarr sees no change in the BSA's reliance on predominantly volunteer leadership, its sponsorship by churches and other community-based organizations, or its local council system.

Will the BSA's programs be substantially different? "I don't think so," Tarr said. "There will still be camping and hiking and outdoor activities, plus hobby and vocational stuff. The vocational aspects will play an increasing part in it—in Boy Scouting as well as in Exploring."

Continuing developments in the patterns of family life and in technology —particularly the computer—are sure to affect Scouting in ways not yet clear. "There's probably going to be more gravitation to the home because of home entertainment and home computers, and because more people

ONE MAN'S VIEW

We've gone through this transition where the Scouts think you've got to have a new sleeping bag and all this other up-to-date stuff, and we forgot the real basics of living close to nature and with nature, and observing nature. You can't blame the kids for that, you can blame us adults.

Of course, when I'm in the woods alone with a fire, I feel closer to the Lord than I do at any other time, and I enjoy this. I think young people enjoy it, too, if we can just get them slowed down enough to do it.

In the last few years, I think, Scouting has been turning around and going back to the old idea of living off the land. We've gotten a lot of old Scouters back in, so we don't have only nuts like me that never got out. It's turning around, and I think we're getting back to the basics and preparing boys to learn to live off the land and respect the land.

—*Walter M. Thomason,*
Tri-State Area Council camping chairman,
Ashland, Ky.

A single mother paddles, her boy enjoys the weekend's surroundings, and a Scouter watches from the stern.

will be working at home hooked up to computers," Tarr predicted. Even so, he believes, there will be no acute shortage of volunteers for Scouting. He expects the BSA to tap the talents and energies of retired persons and the idealism of college students; if anything, he said, the volunteer spirit is going to be stronger.

Over the past 75 years, the Boy Scouts of America has had a significant impact on the lives of millions of Americans and on society as a whole. The most obvious effect has been on the outdoor recreation and environmental movements.

Tens of millions of boys were first introduced to camping, hiking, nature study, and other outdoor activities through Scouting—more than through all other agencies and private camps combined—and it is certain that former Scouts have been in the vanguard of both the camping boom and the environmental movement. Throughout its history (long before terms like ecology and environmental science entered the common tongue) the Boy Scouts of America has been a leader in conservation. It could not have been otherwise, with pioneer conservationists like Theodore Roosevelt, Gifford Pinchot, and William T. Hornaday among Scouting's earliest advocates. Scouts have planted millions of trees, built and set out thousands of birdhouses and mammal-nesting boxes, and completed countless other projects. In recent years, in reponse to the call for energy conservation, Scouting units have become leaders in waste collection for recycling.

The Boy Scouts of America has also left its mark by training millions of youths in first aid. Hundreds of lives have been saved and serious injuries alleviated because Scouts and former Scouts knew what to do in an emergency. Each year, the BSA's National Court of Honor bestows about 175 Medals of Merit for exceptional service, usually involving first aid or other emergency skills. In addition, the Court annually honors an average of 65 Scouts and Scouters for heroism in saving life.

Many American men (and of late, women, too) have found their life's work through Scouting. A deliberate effort is made in Exploring nowadays to expose young people to careers, but Boy Scouting's merit-badge offerings have had the same effect ever since 1910. Many astronomers, foresters, geologists, naturalists, scientists, photographers, and men in skilled trades owe their initiation into their careers to a Boy Scout merit badge.

Scouting's effects cannot be isolated from those of home, school, church, peer group, and the myriad other influences that shape character and personality. Nevertheless, most old Scouts and veteran Scouters are prepared to swear that the values they absorbed in Scouting, by precept and by the example of admired and often beloved leaders, have guided them through life. Almost 300 men and a few women whose roots in Scouting go back 40, 50, even 75 years, were interviewed for this book. With few exceptions, they said that the Scouting experience had shaped their lives.

Seventy-odd million Americans have been members of the BSA since 1910. Many, of course, were touched only superficially by Scouting's principles. Still, a great number of them have striven to make those ideals their guideposts for life. Their very striving has made America a better place for all her people.

Jamborees:
Scouting on Parade

Trading patches was a favorite activity at the 1981 national jamboree.

Big Guns on Opening Day

A 21-cannon salute and a stirring program of loud, live music launched the BSA's 1981 national jamboree, at Fort A. P. Hill, in Virginia. Twenty-seven thousand Scouts had traveled from all over the United States to participate in the week-long gathering, the tenth in American Scouting's history, and at least one person present had attended the very first national jamboree, in 1937—Chief Scout Executive Jim Tarr, who had been an Eagle Scout at the time. The myriad activities at Fort A. P. Hill ranged from recreating the Brownsea Island Camp and competing at archery and canoeing to attending seminars on careers in communications and Scouting. The location, in the Tidewater area of Virginia, proved so ideal that it was selected for the BSA's 75th anniversary jamboree, in July of 1985, which is expected to be the biggest one ever.

Scouting leaders including Chief Scout Executive Tarr, second from left, give the Scout salute during 1981 jamboree opening-day ceremonies. The bands that performed included a 1,700-piece harmonica ensemble composed of Scouts from Ohio and West Virginia.

Scouts From Near and Far

"I want to go canoeing!" said one Scout from New Mexico as soon as he reached the 1981 jamboree site. But the first order of business was to set up camp at one of 18 areas (called subcamps) arranged by national region. Every troop had been preparing for the jamboree for months, so confusion was kept to a minimum. For the first time in Scouting history, scheduling of the hundreds of events was handled by computer—soon after arriving at Fort A. P. Hill, each troop received a printout listing the activities prepared for each of its patrols. The jamboree's official theme was Scouting's Reunion With History, and a special Heritage Trail led Scouts through activities from the past including using branding irons and learning Indian crafts. Some troops visited historic sites along the way to Fort A. P. Hill, and one, from San Diego, found that the greatest challenge had been "staying one night in New York."

Scouts from Utah, left, show off their pins, badges, and the new uniforms designed by Oscar de la Renta. Below, a newly arrived Scout orients himself.

Gateways to Friendship

During the 1981 jamboree, Fort A. P. Hill became the site of dozens of elaborate gateways erected by the Scouts to identify their subcamp. One group recreated an old fishing village; another constructed the entrance to a bygone town on the prairie. An Ohio Scout whose troop made an airplane of lashed wood and plastic remarked, "We would really like to take the gateway home, but we don't know if we'll be able to untie all the knots."

A frontier-wagon entranceway welcomes visitors to a Utah troop's campsite.

One of the 230 Scouts at the 1981 jamboree displays his patrol's guidepost.

Boy Scouts from Kansas constructed this homemade wood-and-rope Ferris wheel.

Sunfish scoot across the waters at Moraine State Park, in Pennsylvania, during the 1977 national jamboree. Usually staged once every 4 years, in the year after a presidential

election, jamborees have been held at sites all across the country—from California (1953) and Idaho (1969) to Valley Forge (1964).

A line of Scouts compete at archery at the 1981 jamboree.

As troop mates shout encouragement, Scouts hold a tug of war.

Contests and Challenges

The vast setting of the 1981 jamboree—it measured about 12 miles by 15 miles—was packed with activities for Scouts. "I was a bit scared," one boy admitted about being faced with the Confidence Course. The challenge there included walking over a rope bridge, swinging over an "alligator pit," and then sliding down a long rail, but the Scout's abilities (and the course's built-in safety features) brought him through. Some tests emphasized group rather than individual achievement—the Heritage Trail demanded that a troop carry a 240-pound log over a series of obstacles. Remarked the trail boss, "If the boys expect a history quiz, they're in for a shock."

Along the Awareness Trail, Scouts learn what it's like to play volleyball in a wheelchair.

Scouts found time for washing and drying between their many jamboree activities.

Wearing a souvenir hat from Puerto Rico, a young chef demonstrates his skill with a spatula.

Above, Scouts peer out of a special tank brought to the jamboree for snorkel instruction. Below, a Scout is clean.

Safety in Numbers

Enough pancakes to tower a mile high and nearly 1.8 million slices of bread were among the food consumed by Scouts and Scouters at the 1981 jamboree. Troops cooked their own food, using 1.7 million pounds of charcoal —special instructions had been issued for banging together charcoal-burning stoves. To wash all that food down, a quart of milk and pint of fruit juice daily per Scout were provided. Also provided in bulk was advice for dealing with the outdoor realities of midsummer Virginia. "Stay off all bridges during electrical storms." "Leaflets three, let it be." "Attached ticks can be removed with a pair of tweezers." To the surprise of few, every Scout and Scouter survived. Not all of the trading post's merchandise made it, though; completely gone by the week's end were neckerchief slides, hat pins, insulated mugs, charms, and T-shirts.

237

The Great Night

Each national jamboree ends in a grand finale, with a massive show on the last evening. In 1981, the entertainment included a parade of every patrol flag at the jamboree, a 20-minute pyrotechnical display that sent up nearly 5 tons of fireworks, performances by Burl Ives and the Oak Ridge Boys, and a multimedia show that included videotaped highlights of the week's happenings. In the cold light of dawn, the BSA began interviewing Scouts and Scout leaders in a study to determine whether the jamboree had truly been worthwhile and whether the tradition was worth continuing. When all was said and done, the answer was clear—and the theme for the 1985 jamboree will be, appropriately, The Spirit Lives On.

Bob Hope, opposite, was the leading entertainer at the 1977 jamboree. The fireworks display at the 1981 jamboree, below, was the most spectacular of all jamborees.

GLOSSARY OF SCOUTING TERMS

Advisor, Explorer. A man or woman (21 or older) who works with an Explorer post.

Akela. Term of respect in Cub Scouting; may refer to a Cub Scout leader, parent, teacher, etc. The name comes from Rudyard Kipling's *Jungle Book*.

Alpha Phi Omega (APO). A college service organization made up primarily of former and current members of BSA.

Baden-Powell, Robert S. S. Founder of the worldwide Scouting movement.

boatswain. The elected youth leader of a Sea Explorer ship.

Boy Scout. Registered youth member of a Boy Scout troop. He must have completed the fifth grade and be at least 10½ years old or be 11 years old. He must not yet be 18. "Scout" is synonymous.

Boy Scouts of America. Legal name of Scouting's organization in the USA. Abbreviated BSA.

Boys' Life. Monthly magazine of the Boy Scouts of America.

BSA alumni family. An association for all former youth or adult members of the BSA.

camporee. District or council campout.

chartered organization. A religious, civic, fraternal, community, educational, or other entity chartered by the BSA to operate a pack, troop, post, or ship.

Chief Scout Executive. The top professional officer of the BSA.

commissioner. A volunteer Scouter who is the "quality control" person for the program at the unit, district, or council level.

crew. The working group within a Sea Explorer ship; similar to a Cub Scout den or Scout patrol.

Cub Scout. Registered youth member of a Cub Scout pack. He must have completed second grade and be from 7 to 10 years old.

Cub Scout Promise. "I (name) promise to do my best to do my duty to God and my country, to help other people, and to obey the Law of the Pack."

Cubmaster. An adult, 21 or older, who leads a Cub Scout pack.

den. Subdivision of a Cub Scout pack, usually with six to 10 boys.

den chief. Scout or Explorer who assists a Cub Scout den leader.

den leader. An adult who supervises a Cub Scout den.

denner. Cub Scout or Webelos Scout elected by his peers to help the den leader.

Distinguished Eagle Award. Presented to Eagle Scouts (at least 25 years after earning Eagle Award) who have distinguished themselves in a career or public life.

district executive. A professional Scouter responsible for a district (geographical entity) within a local council.

Eagle Award. The highest recognition for Scouts.

Explorer. A registered member of a post. He or she is 14 and has completed the eighth grade, or is 15 or older and in any grade; membership may continue up to age 21.

Explorer Code. "As an Explorer—I believe that America's strength lies in her trust in God and in the courage and strength of her people. I will, therefore, be faithful in my religious duties and will maintain a sense of personal honor in my own life. I will treasure my American heritage and will do all I can to preserve and enrich it. I will recognize the dignity and worth of my fellowmen and will use fair play and goodwill in dealing with them. I will acquire the Exploring attitude that seeks the truth in all things and adventure on the frontiers of our changing world."

Exploring Executive. A professional who works with explorers.

Exploring Journal. Quarterly magazine for all registered Explorers.

Family Camping Association. To enrich family life through camping together.

Good Turn. A service to others by an individual or Scouting unit.

jamboree. A national or international camp for Scouts.

Law of the Pack. "The Cub Scout follows Akela. The Cub Scout helps the pack go. The pack helps the Cub Scout grow. The Cub Scout gives goodwill."

leadership corps. An optional subdivision of a troop for 14- and 15-year-old Scouts.

local council. An administrative body responsible for Scouting within a designated territory.

Lone Scout. A boy who follows the Boy Scout program as an individual without membership in a troop. There are also Lone Cub Scouts.

mate. In a Sea Explorer ship, the adult assistant to the Skipper.

merit badge. An award to a Scout for completing requirements in one of more than 100 career and hobby fields.

National Council. The corporate entity of the BSA; it is made up of local council representatives, members at large, and honorary members.

National Court of Honor. A committee of the Boy Scouts of America responsible for administering lifesaving and meritorious conduct awards and other recognitions.

National Eagle Scout Association (NESA). An association for Scouts and former Scouts who have earned the Eagle Award.

Order of the Arrow. Scouting's national brotherhood of honor campers which promotes Scouting's outdoor programs.

pack. The unit that conducts the Cub Scout program for the chartered organization.

patrol. Subdivision of a Boy Scout troop, usually with five to 10 members.

patrol leader. The elected leader of a patrol.

post. The unit that conducts the Explorer program for the chartered organization.

pow wow. A one-day training conference for Cub Scout leaders.

President of BSA. Top elected volunteer.

president, Explorer post. The elected leader of a post.

Quartermaster. The highest award in Sea Exploring.

rank. In Scouting, positions or degrees earned by passing tests. The six ranks are Tenderfoot, Second Class, First Class, Star, Life, and Eagle.

region. One of six geographical administrative units of the BSA: Northeast, Southeast, East Central, North Central, South Central, and Western.

roundtable. A program-planning and morale-building meeting of adult leaders, usually monthly.

Scout executive. The professional staff leader of a local council.

Scout Oath or Promise. "On my honor I will do my best to do my duty to God and my country and to obey the Scout Law; to help other people at all times; to keep myself physically strong, mentally awake, and morally straight."

Scouter. A registered adult member of the BSA.

Scouting **magazine.** Published six times a year for Scouters.

Scoutmaster. The registered adult male leader (at least 21 years old) of a Boy Scout troop.

Sea Explorer. A registered member of a Sea Explorer ship.

senior patrol leader. The key elected boy leader, who helps the Scoutmaster administer a troop.

ship. The unit that conducts the Sea Explorer program for the chartered organization.

Skipper. The adult leader (Advisor) of a Sea Explorer ship.

Tiger Cub. A boy who is 7 years old and in the second grade who, with an adult member of his family, participates in monthly activities with other Tiger Cubs.

troop. The unit that conducts the Boy Scout program for the chartered organization.

unit committee. A group of men and women appointed by the chartered organization to adminster the affairs of its pack, troop, post or ship.

Varsity Scout. A registered youth member of a Varsity Scout team. He is between 14 and 17 years old.

Webelos Scout. A Cub Scout who is 10 years old and is preparing to become a Boy Scout. His den is led by an adult male.

World Friendship Fund. Administered by the Boy Scouts of America to aid Scout associations around the world.

CHRONOLOGY

1910
- *February 8*—Boy Scouts of America incorporated by William D. Boyce in Washington, D.C.

- *May 3*—Boyce accepts offer of help from YMCA officials in organizing BSA.

- *June 1*—National office opened in a New York YMCA.

- *June 21*—Organizational meeting called by YMCA's Edgar M. Robinson.

- *August*—First BSA manual published: *Boy Scouts of America: A Handbook of Woodcraft, Scouting, and Life-craft*, by Ernest Thompson Seton.

- *August 16—September 1*—First BSA camp held at Silver Bay, Lake George, N.Y.

- *October 27*—Board of Managers (National Executive Board) takes title to the Boy Scouts of America from William D. Boyce.

- *November 22*—Colin B. Livingstone elected president pro-tem of the BSA.

1911
- *January 2*—James E. West becomes the first Chief Scout Executive and opens national office at 200 Fifth Avenue, New York City.

- *Spring*—Scout Oath and Law, advancement requirements, badges, and uniforms developed.

- *August 31*—First edition of the *Handbook for Boys* published.

- First Honor Medal for lifesaving presented by National Court of Honor to Charles Scruggs of Cuero, Tex.

- Sea Scouting begun by Arthur A. Carey of Waltham, Mass., using his schooner *Pioneer*; became an official program in 1912.

1912
- First National Good Turn—promotion of "Safe and Sane Fourth of July."

- *July*—BSA publishes its first issue of *Boys' Life*; the magazine had been started in March 1911 by a Rhode Island Boy Scout.

- *Labor Day*—First Eagle Scout badge awarded to Arthur R. Eldred of Troop 1, Oceanside, N.Y.

1913
- Registration of Boy Scouts started; annual fee was 25 cents.

- Regional supervision of local councils started.

- *April 15*—First issue of *Scouting* magazine.

- First *Handbook for Scoutmasters* published in proof edition.

- Church of Jesus Christ of Latter-day Saints becomes first religious body to adopt Scouting.

1914
- Troop committee plan created.

- First William T. Hornaday gold medal for conservation presented.

1915
- Department of Education established for training of Scouters.

- *July 16*—First Order of the Arrow members inducted.

1916
- *June 15*—BSA granted a federal charter protecting its name and insignia.

- First 57 merit badge booklets published.

- National Department of Camping established.

- Pioneer Scouting program adopted for rural boys.

1917
- BSA begins home-front service with entry of United States into World War I.

1918
- By war's end November 11, Boy Scouts had sold more than $200 million worth of Liberty Loan bonds and war stamps; distributed 30 million pieces of government literature; collected 100 railroad cars of nut hulls and peach pits for gas mask manufacture; located 21 million board feet of black walnut trees for gunstocks and airplane propellers; and planted 12,000 gardens.

- Rotary International becomes first service club to adopt Scouting.

1920
- First National Training Conference held for professional Scouters.

- BSA sent 301 Scouts and leaders to first International Jamboree in England.

1922
- Order of the Arrow becomes official program experiment.

1924
- Lone Scouts of America, which had been founded by William D. Boyce in 1915, absorbed by BSA.

- First achievement badges awarded to physically handicapped Scouts.

1926
- First Silver Buffalo awards given by National Council for distinguished service to boyhood.

- Development of program for younger boys authorized.

1927
- Eight Sea Scouts go with Borden-Field Museum expedition to the Bering Sea.

- Inter-Racial Service established to promote Scouting among blacks and other minorities.

1928
- Three Scouts accompany Martin Johnson expedition to Africa.

- Sea Scout Paul A. Siple goes with Byrd expedition to Antarctica.

1929
- *August*—Cubbing program for younger boys begins as pilot project in several cities.

1930
- *April 1*—First Cub Scout pack charters issued.

1931
- Boy Scouts begin Depression relief work with local collections of clothing and food.

- First Silver Beaver awards given for distinguished service to boyhood within local councils.

1932
- Mortimer L. Schiff Scout Reservation in Mendham, N.J., donated by family of late BSA president.

1933
- Explorer Scout program authorized.

1934
- National Good Turn for the needy at request of President Franklin D. Roosevelt; 1.8 million articles of clothing, food, furnishings collected.

1937
- First national jamboree held in Washington, D.C.

1938 • Waite Phillips, Tulsa, Okla., oilman and philanthropist, gives 36,000 acres near Cimarron, N. Mex., for development of Philturn Rockymountain Scoutcamp (now Philmont Scout Ranch).

1940 • Experimental projects to bring Scouting to urban low-income areas begin with money from the Irving Berlin Fund, which was established with royalties from Berlin's song, "God Bless America."

1941 • April-September—Scouts distributed pledge cards and posters advertising Defense Bonds and Stamps, and collected 10.5 million tons of scrap aluminum, 50 million tons of wastepaper.

• After Pearl Harbor, December 7, BSA pledged full support for the war effort. On December 13, Scouts distributed air raid posters.

1942 • For the war effort, Scouts collected scrap rubber, metals, wastepaper, used books, and musical instruments for military camps; distributed government posters and circulars; built model planes and ships for military training; and planted Victory Gardens.

• Air Scouting program begins.

1943 • BSA continued home-front service.

• First Silver Antelope awards presented for distinguished service to boyhood within a region.

1944 • BSA continued home-front service.

• World Friendship Fund established originally to aid Scout associations in wartorn nations.

1945 • Scouts continued home-front service; by the end of World War II in August, the BSA had responded to 69 requests from the government 1941–45.

1949 • Membership age minimums lowered to 8 for Cub Scouts, 11 for Boy Scouts, 14 for Explorers. All boys 14 and over were designated as Explorers; they might remain in a Scout troop as members of an Explorer crew or join a separate post.

1950 • Second national jamboree held at Valley Forge, Pa.

1951 • Two million pounds of clothing collected for foreign and domestic relief.

1952 • Thirty million Liberty Bell doorknob hangers were distributed by 1.8 million BSA members in get-out-the-vote campaign.

1953 • Third national jamboree held at the Irvine Ranch in southern California.

1954 • In National Conservation Good Turn, BSA members undertook thousands of projects for conservation of soil and water, forests and wildlife.

1956 • BSA members distributed 36 million doorknob hangers and 1.3 million posters in get-out-the-vote campaign.

1957 • Fourth national jamboree held at Valley Forge, Pa.

1958 • In National Safety Good Turn, BSA members distributed 50,000 posters and delivered 40 million Civil Defense emergency handbooks.

• Explorer Richard Lee Chappel went with National Academy of Sciences team to Antarctica for International Geophysical Year.

1959 • Special-interest Exploring begins. Boys 14 and older who remained in Scout troops were again designated Boy Scouts, not Explorers.

1960 • Fifth national jamboree held at Colorado Springs, Colo.

• BSA held its third get-out-the-vote Good Turn.

• Johnston Historical Museum opened at national headquarters, North Brunswick, N.J.

1961 • Urban Relationships Service established to replace Inter-Racial Service; pilot projects begin in public housing.

1962 • First National Explorer Delegate Conference held at Ann Arbor, Mich.

1964 • Sixth national jamboree held at Valley Forge, Pa.

1965 • Inner-City Rural Program launched.

1967
- BSA hosted 12th world jamboree at Farragut State Park, Idaho.

- Ernest Thompson Seton Memorial Library and Museum at Philmont Scout Ranch and the Ellsworth H. Augustus International Scout House at national headquarters were opened.

- Cub Scouting program revised; Webelos Scouting established for 10-year-old boys.

1969
- Girls permitted to join special-interest Explorer posts.

- Seventh national jamboree held at Farragut State Park, Idaho.

1970
- First National Explorer Olympics held at Colorado State University.

- Project SOAR (Save Our American Resources), a continuing conservation Good Turn, was launched.

1971
- Operation Reach, a national program against drug abuse, was started.

- First National Explorer Presidents Congress held in Washington, D.C.

- *Exploring* magazine begins publication.

- First Silver World awards presented by BSA for distinguished service to youth on an international scale.

1972
- Sweeping revisions of the Boy Scout program made; outdoor skills no longer required for advancement to First Class; *Scout Handbook* published.

- National Eagle Scout Association (NESA) founded.

1973
- Eighth national jamboree held at two sites—Moraine State Park in Pennsylvania and Farragut State Park, Idaho.

1976
- Seven hundred and fifty Eagle Scouts and leaders camped all summer on the Mall in Washington to observe nation's bicentennial.

1977
- Ninth national jamboree held at Moraine State Park, Pa.

- Energy conservation emphasized in Project SOAR.

1978
- Age restrictions removed for severely handicapped members, permitting them to earn badges beyond usual requirements.

- Boy Scout advancement plan modified to again require outdoor skills for First Class rank.

- Eagle Scout Mark Leinmiller accompanied National Science Foundation team to Antarctica.

1979
- National office moved to Irving, Tex.

- *The Official Boy Scout Handbook*, reflecting return to outdoor emphasis, was published.

1980
- BSA members distributed fliers advertising national census.

1981
- Tenth national jamboree held at Fort A. P. Hill, Va.

- Hispanic Outreach initiated nationally.

1982
- Tiger Cubs a BSA program begins for 7-year-old boys and adult family members.

- Bear Cub Scout advancement plan enhanced.

- Career awareness Exploring becomes official.

- "Prepared for Today" program started for "latchkey children."

Colin H. Livingstone

James J. Storrow

Milton A. McRae

Walter W. Head

Mortimer L. Schiff

Amory Houghton

John M. Schiff

Ellsworth H. Augustus

Irving Feist

Kenneth K. Bechtel

Thomas J. Watson, Jr.

Norton Clapp

BSA NATIONAL PRESIDENTS

Colin B. Livingstone	1910–25
James J. Storrow	1925–26
Milton A. McRae	1926★
Walter W. Head	1926–31
Mortimer L. Schiff	1931★
Walter W. Head	1931–46
Amory Houghton	1946–51
John M. Schiff	1951–56
Kenneth K. Bechtel	1956–59
Ellsworth H. Augustus	1959–64
Thomas J. Watson, Jr.	1964–68
Irving I. Feist	1968–71
Norton Clapp	1971–73
Robert W. Reneker	1973–75
Arch Monson, Jr.	1975–77
Downing B. Jenks	1977–79
John D. Murchison	1979★
Downing B. Jenks	1979–80
Dr. Thomas D. MacAvoy, Ph.D.	1980–82
Edward C. Joullian III	1982–84
Sanford N. McDonnell	1984–

★ Died in office

Robert W.
Reneker

Arch
Monson, Jr.

Downing B.
Jenks

John D.
Murchison

Dr. Thomas C.
MacAvoy

Edward C.
Joullian

Sanford N.
McDonnell

CHIEF SCOUT EXECUTIVES

Dr. James E. West	1911–43
Dr. Elbert K. Fretwell	1943–48
Dr. Arthur A. Schuck	1948–60
Joseph A. Brunton, Jr.	1960–67
Alden G. Barber	1967–76
Harvey L. Price	1976–79
J. L. Tarr	1979–84

Dr. James E. West

Dr. Elbert K. Fretwell

Dr. Arthur A. Schuck

Joseph A. Brunton, Jr.

Alden G. Barber

Harvey L. Price

J. L. Tarr

BSA MEMBERSHIP

Year	Tiger Cubs	Youth Members		Adult Members	Total Membership
		Cub Scouts	Boy Scouts and Explorers		
1915			143,782	38,521	182,303
1920			376,537	114,374	490,911
1930		5,102*	623,382	218,567	847,051
1940		195,369	910,572	343,471	1,449,412
1950		828,344	1,243,305	723,573	2,795,222
1960		1,865,120	1,917,953	1,377,885	5,160,958
1970		2,438,009	2,244,649	1,604,620	6,287,278
1980		1,688,193	1,491,446	1,117,057	4,296,696
1983	123,643**	1,568,799	1,874,772	1,121,754	4,688,968

*new in 1930
**new in 1982

✠ INDEX ✠

Picture Credits

Except for those listed below all credits are courtesy of Boy Scouts of America. Pictures for illustrations from left to right are separated by semicolons; from top to bottom, by dashes.

18–George Eastman House. 18, 19–Massillon Museum. 24–Bettmann Archives. 50, 51–Library of Congress. 80–Library of Congress. 65–Art Shay. 70–M. V. Rubio. 73, 73–Art Shay. 78, 79–Dick Stone of Stone/Clark Productions (Courtesy of Foote, Cone & Belding). 87–Library of Congress. 92, 93–L'Illustration, May 1917. 96–Courtesy of (old) LIFE Magazine. 102, 103–Edward De Courcy. 104–Tidewater Council #596/B.S.A. 136–William Hillcourt. 152, 153–Michigan Historical Collection. 155–Passaic Council/B.S.A 162, 163–Chicksaw Council #558/B.S.A. 164–© MCMLXV Walt Disney Productions. 168, 169–Edwin T. Williams. 175a–Matt Bradley. 192–Vince Heptig. 193–Dan McCoy/Rainbow. 195–Mike Smith/Black Star. 197–Matt Bradley. 200–Northeast Regional Council/B.S.A. 206, 207–Matt Bradley. 208–Roy Zalesky/Black Star. 209–David Falconer. 210–Bob Krist. 212, 213–Vince Heptig. 214–Stephen Kelly. 215–Art Shay. 216–Bob Krist. 218–Scott Witte 1983. 219–David Falconer. 220–Bob Krist. 222, 223–Roy Zalesky/Black Star.

Acknowledgements

A book attempting to tell the 75-year story of a movement that has engaged the attention of 70 million Americans cannot be a one-man enterprise. The author had the full cooperation of the National Office of the Boy Scouts of America, and many staff members gave their help. Particularly valuable was the assistance of Librarian Ann L. McVicar, Library Clerk Barbara J. Maier, Archivist Betty Newton, whose formal title is manager of Records Management, and Joan McLachlan of her office. In addition, Mike Roytek, photo editor at the BSA deserves thanks for researching many of the pictures in this book with unfailing good humor and cheer.

Nearly 300 men and women who have been active in Scouting throughout much of its history in America were interviewed for this book. With few exceptions, they have from 40 to 75 years of tenure in Scouting. Not all of them are quoted directly, but each one contributed to the mosaic of memories of what Scouting was like from 1910 through the 1970's. They are:

Harold Adams, Elmer H. Allen, Orange E. Apple, Walker Armington, III, E.W. Armistead, Carlton M. Armour, Paul Ashley, Earl E. Bagley, Arthur Wm. Barrett, John H. Bayless, Douglas Beals, Henry W. Behrens, W.E. Bennington, Maj. Earl B. Benton (Ret.), J. Ersol Berchtold, Edward R. Berger, Herbert R. Bieri, Herbert Birch, Leo O. Blake, Cmdr. James M. Blakeman (Ret.), Albert W. Boehnlein, R.J. Bohner, Milton H. Book, Don J. Breining, Edgar Z. Briggs, Jr., John D. Briggs, John W. Briggs, Joseph H. Brinton, Alexander Britton, Henry N. Brown, III, Harold K. Brown, Harvey Burle, Edwin Burnham, M. Dean Burns, Wally Bushnick, Edwin Buthmann, LeRoy N. Butler;

Joseph W. Cafmeyer, Howard Carl, Gilbert W. Carlin, Herb Carr, James M. Carroll, Fielding Chandler, Raul A. Chavez, Otis H. Chidester, Richard T. Clarke, Arthur J.H. Clement, Jr., Rev. John D. Clinton, Frederic J. Closser, Henry Gardner Colby, Murray Cole, William Coles, Jr., Robert C. Colyar, Joe Cooke, Thomas R. Costello, A.E. Cunliff, Howard Cunningham, Ben Dahlman, Loy W. Davis, Willard H. Davis, Sr., Earl Day, Al R. Dayes, Hazen A. Dean, Edward DeCourcy, Mitchell Diamond, Lester W. Dilts, Frank Dix, Harold E. Donahue, G.H. Donaldson, W.R. Donaldson, John Lewis Dowell, Jr., Albert Drompp, C.E. Dunlap, Jr.;

Lester Eastham, Dr. William W. Edel, Harold Edwards, Robert Edwards, Fred C. Eggers, Harold O. Evans, E.S. Ewing, Dr. Irving M. Falkenbury, Ray O. Fann, Leonard Filson, Lt. Col. Jay N. Fisher (Ret.), Michael Fisher, Glenford J. Foster, Carl Fowls, Arnold Joseph Frankel, Frederick Franzwick, William S. Frey, James Fritze, Len Fuchs, Edward P. Fuller, Robert Galen, Saul Gilbert, Joseph B. Gill, William Glover, John L. Godsey, Allen Goldblatt, Arthur Goostree, Gordon Gourley, Perry B. Green, Norman A. Greist;

Robert Haas, Oakley V. Haight, Jr., Robert W. Haley, Eberhard Hamer, Harry Hansen, Fred J. Harm, Ben Havilland, Charles M. Heistand, Dan O. Henry, John B. Hill, William Hillcourt, Donald C. Hoffman, Lawrence S. Hogle, Charles S. Hollander, Robert Hooks, George W. Hoover, Sr., Louis A. Hornbeck, Ariel L. Hoth, Jack V. Howard, J.F. Hughes, J.E. Hullander, William L. Imerschein, Jack W. Isenberg, Robert Jensen, John L. Johnson, John Johnston, Starr West Jones, John J. Jordan, Walter F. Josti;

Kurttle J. Karlinsey, O.K. Kaslin, John R. Kellogg, Sr., J. Harvey Kellow, Bill Kennah, Knight B. Kerr, Dr. Frank H. Kidd, Jr., John Kilgore, Roy E. Kimpel, Louis A. Klewer, Robert C. Koerner, Kenneth J. Koob, Victor Kotter, Stephen L. Kowalski, William D. Krebs, Henry G. Kreiner, Dr. Stanley Kuffel, Richard F. Kurr, John P. L'Abbe, A.L. Larsen, Alex Lea, Mary Gene Lea, Alan N. Lobeck, Francis E. Logan, George Loriot, Bill B. Lowlar, Vern Luby, Frank Lutz;

J. Edward Mack, Christian K. Madison, Bill Marsden, Howard T. Mason, Cecil F. Matson, Thomas May, A.G. McGuire, Bill McManus, Walter F. McManus, Thomas S. Merola, Rev. Herman A. Meyer, Edward S. Miller, Tuskahoma Brown Miller, Herbert S. Miner, Capt. Alexander N. Moffatt (Ret.), Warren F. Morgan, Harold Morse, Frederick E. Munich, Henry A. Murray, Anthony Myers, Carl Myers, Ann W. Nally, H. Banks Newman, Rea A. Nunnallee, John Oberer, Col. Charles Carlton Oldham, Vern L. Orth;

Leighton (Andy) Parezo, Frank Parr, Gus Parthesius, Albert W. Patzlaff, Ivo V. Pennington, Bent V. Petersen, Fran Petersen, Carl R. Peterson, Clarence E. Peterson, Ralph W. Peterson, Joseph D. Pickle, Lawrence Portanova, M. Norman Powell, Charles Preyer, James W. Price, LeRoy W. Pritchard, Rear Adm. Schuyler N. Pyne (Ret.), Sidney Quinby, Charles Ragland, Clark A. Ralph, Col. Lloyd Rall (Ret.), Laurence Raymer, Edward L. Reilly, Robert F. Ritchie, Joseph F. Robinson, Charles C. Roessler, Cecil Rogers, Ray D. Rogers, Dr. H.H. Rose, Gerald Rowe, Everett M. Royce, William D. Russell;

Yale L. Saffro, Julian H. Salomon, Wayne Sanderson, Charles H. Saunders, Frank Scalise, LeRoy Schuppert, LeGrande G. Sharp, Frank T. Sharpe, William Shaw, Melvin A. Shikes, Paul W. Shogren, Harold J. Short, John Slegelmilch, Sr., John Slegelmilch, Jr., Morris Slotkin, Philip M. Smart, Arthur Smith, Edward A. Smith, Wilbur Smith, F. Jay Snover, Rod Speirs, Edmund D. Strang, Mrs. Walter M. Steele, Sr., Sylvan P. Stern, Robert Stetson, A.J. Stilwell, Bob Stohlman, Frank M. Stone, Thornton F. Stone, Lt. Gen. Daniel B. Strickler (Ret.);

C.W. Tacke, Albert E. Tarbox, James L. Tarr, Alfred Taylor, Sr., Walter M. Thomason, Claude Thompson, Duane Tooley, G. Malcolm Townsley, Quentin Tracy, Paul B. Trubey, William J. Tucker, Walter R. Turner, Theodore F. Tuttle, William Tweeddale, E. Royal Van Der Hoef, Bill Van Slyke, Billy Jim Vaughn, Mance H. Vaught, Paul S. Von Bacho, Charles Wandel, Dr. Wallace Watt, Julien Wayne, James Weeks, Harry Weiner, Donald Weren, Joseph W. White, Richard Whitney, Roger Whitworth, Marvin Wiemers, Dr. Edwin T. Williams, George M. Williams, F.D. Williamson, Jr., Glenn S. Williamson, Henry M. Wilson, Floyd P. Wolfarth, Joseph D. Wooding, Newton Woodruff, C. Brower Woodward, Charles H.F. Wright, Fred A. Zimmann.

Contributing memorabilia, written reminiscences of Scouting and Lone Scouting, and histories of local Scout councils and long-tenured troops were: Kenneth Arnold, O.A. Batcheller, Frances L. Bennett, John L. Briggs, Richard Conklin, Albert R. Crocker, James H. Delk, Lewis Dulaney, Andrew F. Fitzhugh, Richard B. Eaton, Albion Ende, Ernest L. Gambell, M.F. Gilmer, John W. Hanks, Howard Holcombe, Rev. Dr. Byron D. Hughes, Martin Krueger, Thomas F. Lehmier, Dr. Harry N. March, Joseph Morris, Elmer P. Pelton, Julius L. Piland, O.C. (Sam) Rankin, Dick Raymond, Wayne E. Rosenoff (who loaned tape-recorded reminiscences by Lionel Chute), David E. Setzer, Walter Smith, Herbert Stamer, Rev. Walter M. Steele, Jr., Harry B. Walton, Sr., Beaumert Whitton, and Edgar B. Wicklander. Ellie Murphy, assistant director of the YMCA of the USA Development Center, provided biographical material about Edgar M. Robinson.

Finally, the author is indebted to Russell Bourne and Connie Roosevelt of American Heritage Books, who know wheat from chaff and how to winnow.

rockets
through
SPACE